ICT AND SPECIAL
EDUCATIONAL NEEDS

Learning and Teaching with Information and Communications Technology

Series editors: Anthony Adams and Sue Brindley

The role of ICT in the curriculum is much more than simply a passing trend. It provides a real opportunity for teachers of all phases and subjects to rethink fundamental pedagogical issues alongside the approaches to learning that pupils need to apply in classrooms. In this way it foregrounds the way in which teachers can match in school the opportunities for learning provided in home and community. The series is firmly rooted in practice and also explores the theoretical underpinning of the ways in which curriculum content and skills can be developed by the effective integration of ICT in schooling. It addresses the educational needs of the early years, the primary phase and secondary subject areas. The books are appropriate for pre-service teacher training and continuing professional development as well as for those pursuing higher degrees in education.

Published and forthcoming titles:

R. Barton (ed.): *Learning and Teaching Science with ICT*
L. Florian and J. Hegarty (eds): *ICT and Special Educational Needs*
A. Loveless and B. Dore (eds): *ICT in the Primary School*
M. Monteith (ed.): *Teaching Primary Literacy with ICT*
J. Way and T. Beardon (eds): *ICT and Primary Mathematics*

ICT AND SPECIAL EDUCATIONAL NEEDS

A tool for inclusion

Edited by
Lani Florian and John Hegarty

Open University Press

Open University Press
McGraw-Hill Education
Shoppenhangers Road
Maidenhead
Berkshire
England
SL6 2QL

email: enquiries@openup.co.uk
world wide web: www.openup.co.uk

First Published 2004

A catalogue record of this book is available from the British Library

ISBN 0 335 2119 5 (pb)   0 335 21196 8 (hb)

Library of Congress Cataloging-in-Publication Data
CIP data applied for

Typeset by RefineCatch Limited, Bungay, Suffolk
Printed in Great Britain by Bell and Bain, Glasgow

CONTENTS

List of contributors   vii
Acknowledgements   x
Series editors' preface   xi

Introduction   1
Lani Florian and John Hegarty

1   Uses of technology that support pupils with special
    educational needs   7
    Lani Florian

2   Information and communications technology, special
    educational needs and schools: a historical perspective of UK
    government initiatives   21
    Chris Stevens

3   From integration to inclusion: using ICT to support learners
    with special educational needs in the ordinary classroom   35
    Lesley Rahamin

4   Using computer-based assessment to identify learning problems   46
    Chris Singleton

5   Integrated learning systems: effects on learning and self-esteem   64
     Ian Hedley

6   A whole-school approach to ICT for children with physical
     disabilities   80
     Clive Lilley

7   Using virtual environments with pupils with learning
     difficulties   96
     Penny Standen and David Brown

8   Managing special educational needs provision with ICT:
     individual education plans and beyond   109
     Allison Rees and Anna Williams

9   Managing innovations in ICT: issues for staff development   128
     John Hegarty

     Index   147

LIST OF CONTRIBUTORS

David Brown, Nottingham Trent University, is Reader in Interactive Systems within the Department of Computing and Mathematics. His primary research interest is in the design, implementation and evaluation of multimedia systems to promote social inclusion. He holds several European and national grant awards in this field and is currently leading research to develop virtual training environments for use by people with a cognitive disability and multimedia systems to develop basic skills in young homeless people, as well as maintaining an ongoing collaborative research programme with Dr Penny Standen. He is also a member of the national steering committee for the British Computer Society Disability Group.

Lani Florian, University of Cambridge, is a lecturer in Special and Inclusive Education specializing in inclusion of pupils with special educational needs in mainstream schools. Her research interests focus on models of provision for meeting special educational needs and teaching practice in inclusive secondary schools. In 1999, she won the NASEN/TES Academic Book Award for Promoting Inclusive Practice (co-edited with C. Tilstone and R. Rose). She is editor of the *Journal of Research in Special Educational Needs*.

Ian Hedley is a teacher and special educational needs coordinator in a mainstream secondary school. In 2001, he received a Masters Degree in

Education from the University of Plymouth. His dissertation examined the effects of Successmaker on pupil achievement.

John Hegarty, Keele University, is Director of the Computer Applications to Special Education (CASE) research unit in the Department of Psychology at Keele University and is Director of the MA in Community Care Learning Disability and the Diploma in Information Technology for People with Special Needs taught courses. He was recently guest editor for a special issue of the *British Journal of Educational Technology* on special needs ICT.

Clive Lilley was appointed to his current post as headteacher of a large special school in North Staffordshire in 1987. The school became one of the first 75 Beacon schools in the country in 1998. This has provided the opportunity to support special needs pupils and teaching and support staff in mainstream and special schools across the region. The school has a reputation for excellence in the use of ICT.

Lesley Rahamin has been a class teacher in London primary schools, worked as a support teacher for learners with special educational needs and an adviser for CENMAC, using IT to support learners with a variety of individual needs. Lesley now works as an Education Consultant promoting good practice in ICT and special educational needs.

Allison Rees has been teaching since 1975. She has taught in both KS1 and KS2 and worked extensively as a learning support teacher. She has acted as an special educational needs advisory teacher for the London Borough of Havering and is currently the special educational needs coordinator for Early Years and KS1 in a large primary school.

Chris Singleton, University of Hull, is Senior Lecturer in Education at the Department of Psychology. His main research interests are in cognitive factors that underlie the development of basic skills (especially literacy) and how these relate to success and failure in education. His research group pioneered the development of computerized diagnostic assessment systems that are now widely used in primary and secondary schools in the UK and elsewhere in the world. He is co-editor of the *Journal of Research in Reading* and also co-editor of the book *Psychological Assessment of Reading* (Routledge, 1997).

Penny Standen, University of Nottingham, is Reader in Health Psychology and Learning Disabilities and is involved in evaluating ways of promoting the independence and quality of life of people with intellectual disabilities. She has been working with Dr David Brown since the early 1990s developing and evaluating virtual environments and multimedia for the training and education of people with intellectual disabilities. They have recently received funding from the ESRC to look at tutoring strategies in virtual environments and from the EPSRC to develop more appropriate devices for interacting with and navigating through virtual environments. She is currently working with switch-controlled software for people with profound and multiple disabilities and is investigating the potential of interactive software to promote cognitive skills.

Chris Stevens, Becta, was appointed to NCET/Becta in February 1996 as Head of Special Educational Needs and Inclusion. Following a long teaching career, he was appointed as Professional Officer for Special Educational Needs at the National Curriculum Council (NCC), later the School Curriculum and Assessment Authority (SCAA). Chris worked at SCAA during the Dearing Review of the National Curriculum and Qualifications and was responsible for extending access both to the curriculum and to recognition of achievement.

Anna Williams is Head of Special Educational Needs Support Service (SENSS) in an outer London Borough. She has worked as a 'class-based' special educational needs coordinator in primary schools. Her current work as the advisory teacher for pupils with physical impairments includes pupils from pre-school to post-16. INSET is a key part of the role of the SENSS team in supporting special educational needs coordinators in meeting the needs of pupils effectively.

ACKNOWLEDGEMENTS

We are grateful to the contributors for their generosity in sharing their work and giving their time to such a long project. Our commissioning editor at the Open University Press, Shona Mullen, has been a delight to work with. Special thanks are due to Paula Peachey and Alison Craig, administrative assistants at the University of Cambridge, who kept us organized and did a brilliant job helping to make sure that the final manuscript met the publisher's criteria for submission. Any errors or omissions are our own despite their best efforts.

Our partners Martyn Rouse and Rosamond Hegarty have been patient, helpful and supportive beyond what should ever be asked.

SERIES EDITORS' PREFACE

If the essence of ICT is its ability to dissolve boundaries, whether between countries or between subject, teacher and learner, then inclusion can be said to be its defining characteristic. Ensuring all students are offered maximum opportunity to succeed, whatever their particular learning needs, is a characteristic of effective teaching in all schools. Inclusion is a broad term and refers to a range of differing types of student need. In this volume, Florian and Hegarty explore the ways in which ICT can afford particular opportunities to those students who need additional support in the classroom – students with special educational needs (SEN).

It could be said that the special educational needs field has walked a tightrope since the publication of the pivotal Warnock Report of 1978, which initiated a clarion call for integration in post-war Britain. Then the introduction of statements of special educational need meant that, in theory at least, the curriculum could, quite rightly, be adapted to the needs of individual pupils. On the other hand, the introduction of the principle of mainstreaming meant that, so far as possible, pupils with special educational needs should be educated as much as possible alongside their peers to the benefit of both groups.

Since that time, policy and provision for learners with special educational needs has developed rapidly. Whereas the 1981 Education Act, which followed the Warnock Report, established the principle of mainstream education for pupils with special educational needs, the Special

Educational Needs and Disability Act of 2001 (SENDA) has established a right to mainstream education for all pupils as schools can no longer refuse a mainstream place to a child with special educational needs.

Hence the importance of the subtitle to the present volume.

The widespread introduction of ICT in schools has made a major impact on the learning patterns of pupils with SEN; indeed, in the early days of IT in schools the Scottish Council for Educational Technology made a special impact in this field. But a 'tool for inclusion' can also be a tool for separation. No-one who has observed at first-hand the work of pupils with severe disabilities working with laptops – with alternative means of input from concept keyboards to the use of 'wands' and voice recognition – can have any doubt of the liberating effect of the new technologies for those pupils whose hand and eye coordination and motor skills would otherwise isolate them from the usual educational process. But laptops, however fashionable they may be now, have their limitations in terms of inclusivity. These include the size of keyboard and screen which means that the laptop is essentially a tool for an individual user, though we have seen some very exciting individual and group work using laptops and wireless technology. 'One on every desk' may be a good slogan for Microsoft and a business environment; but it may be less appropriate in schools.

Therefore, we especially welcome in these pages those chapters that stress and demonstrate the importance of group work where pupils with SEN can be genuinely involved in a process of inclusion. If we put this alongside Warnock's projection that some 40 per cent of pupils will have special educational needs during their school lives, we can see how important this becomes.

What is ultimately important is not the hardware but how it is used, the pedagogy that underlies the classroom world. For example, if we observe pupils working in groups it is the quality of the talk and discussion rather than the control of the keyboard that is paramount. Here SEN students can be empowered to make a fundamental contribution alongside their peers and we are able to see real inclusion demonstrated. But there is still a long way to go. For example, the ubiquity of the internet and web sites raises important issues about appropriate access for blind and partially sighted pupils.

As an Ofsted document, 'Evaluating Education Inclusion: Guidance for Inspectors and Schools' usefully makes clear:

> An educationally inclusive school is one in which the teaching and learning, achievements and attitudes, and well-being of every young person matter. Effective schools are educationally inclusive schools. This shows, not only in their performance, but also in their ethos and their willingness to offer new opportunities to pupils who have experienced previous difficulties. This does not mean treating all pupils in the same way. Rather it involves taking account of pupils' varied life experiences and needs.

We need to go further down the road of 'offer[ing] new opportunities' by exploiting the potential of ICT to enhance the individual learning experiences of all students. If the new technologies are truly to become a 'tool for inclusion', it is important for all teachers to understand the potential of ICT for students with special educational needs. The present volume makes an important contribution in this area and we commend it not only to those who teach in special schools but also to those who teach students with SEN in mainstream classrooms.

Anthony Adams and Sue Brindley

INTRODUCTION

Lani Florian and John Hegarty

This is a book about two complex subjects: the rapidly changing field of information technology and learners with special educational needs (SEN). The term 'special educational needs' is an elusive concept and covers many kinds of difficulties in learning as well as meaning different things to different people in different places. Information and communications technology (ICT) refers to a range of various technologies as well as being a subject of study in its own right. In this book, we examine the intersection of ICT and the field of special educational needs.

As you read the book, there are two important points to keep in mind. First, the term 'special educational needs' covers an array of problems from those arising from particular impairments to those resulting from the complex interaction of pupil and school factors. Learning and behavioural difficulties may be experienced by any learner some of the time. Secondly, not all impairments or disabilities create barriers to learning. One should not assume that disabilities and learning difficulties are concurrent. Nor are they synonymous terms. Many people are disabled by an impairment but they may or may not be *handicapped* by the condition. There are many physical impairments which do not necessarily interfere with learning in school. For example, a learner with spina bifida (the term used to describe people whose spinal columns have not closed properly) may or may not experience difficulties in learning. One cannot assume that spina bifida gives rise to learning difficulties. Nor can one assume that any difficulties the learner is experiencing are directly caused by spina bifida. It may be that the difficulty is indirectly related, as in the case where the learner misses out on teaching because of absence from school.

However, there are some conditions and impairments that are known to create barriers to learning unless accommodations are made. A person with a visual impairment, for example, may need some kind of support or accommodation to achieve the same functioning as a person without the visual impairment. In a lesson that requires access to the World Wide Web, it may be necessary to make an accommodation such as changing the size of the text, the colour of the hyperlink, or adding sound such as a speaking browser. Other accommodations include special keyboards to help children with coordination difficulties, screen-reading software for people with visual disabilities, software to help children with communication difficulties convey choices, and the many software packages that help children practise basic skills in a range of curriculum areas. The extent to which a learner is handicapped by a disability or by circumstance may or may not require such accommodations. There are two reasons for this. One is because the learner's difficulty may not be severe enough to create a barrier to learning. The second is because the support or accommodation that is required to enable the learner to overcome the barrier does not require specialist input. There are many accommodations that can be made by resourceful practitioners. Indeed, one aim of this book is to provide a source of information about ICT and how it can be used to support pupils with SEN. At the same time, the book addresses the topic of specialist knowledge. The intention is to help practitioners understand enough about special educational needs so that they may consider what kinds of support and accommodations they can make on their own and what may be available from specialists.

Information and communications technology and special educational needs

Information and communications technology (ICT) is a useful phrase for summarizing the myriad ways in which microchip technology has permeated many aspects of everyday life, in education, leisure, work and the home. In the National Curriculum, it is a subject in its own right, and children are expected to master a range of computer skills, such as word processing and data handling using spreadsheets. As the interconnectivity of computers has become an everyday fact of life, the 'communications' element has become increasingly important, with more and more use being made in school of the World Wide Web for accessing websites, communication with others by e-mail and videoconferencing.

It is probably fair to say that in many primary and secondary schools ICT is considered an important, although perhaps not essential, part of the life of the school. Cuban (2001) reports that teachers tend to view computers as audiovisual equipment and use them to support rather than drive or determine teaching and learning. Indeed, children appear to use ICT more frequently – and to do more things – at home than at school, where they are likely to have more powerful computers and greater freedom to do with them things that personally interest them. Of course, as already noted, some children will need accommodations (e.g. customized keyboards, voice synthesizers and so on) to have the same access to technology as part of everyday life as do other children.

In contrast to the situation in mainstream schools, ICT in many special schools has become an everyday and essential element of teaching and learning. Clive Lilley's chapter in this volume (Chapter 6) is just one example of a school that has embraced technology for its children – and Lilley conveys the massive change that has occurred in the past 15 years in the life of a special school as a result of the growth in microtechnology and related applications. Moreover, as several chapters in this book explore, this growth in the applications of technology has had implications for pupils with SEN in mainstream schools as well.

The reason for the importance of ICT in special needs education is a consequence of the many innovations that have occurred in the ways in which technology can support children with special needs. Children without disabilities require few modifications of any standard computer package that one can purchase in high street shops for home use. Even very young children can access their favourite software package with relatively little adult help. But this is not true of many children with disabilities, for whom modifications are not only desirable but essential.

The present volume is a showcase for these many applications. We hope that it will be a systematic introduction for teachers new to working with children with special needs, as well as an interesting update for those familiar with the area. A theme that runs throughout the book is the essential role that teachers have in enabling effective ICT use for children. It is easy to be impressed by new technology. The combination of novelty and manufacturers' hype can be very attractive to teachers frustrated with the progress some children are able to make. Perhaps the 'latest device', seen perhaps at a computer show, is the answer that has long been sought for a group of children who appear not to be benefiting from what is currently available. The reality in school is very different. The technology does nothing on its own but rather needs to be made to work in practice by the skill and perseverance of the school team.

The organization of this book

This book focuses on how teachers can use microtechnology to support learning. The chapters are written by researchers and practitioners. They offer the researchers' vision of how ICT might be used alongside the practitioners' day-to-day concerns and needs. The chapters of the book are organized around the development of ICT and its effect on provision for pupils with special educational needs. Chapter 1 considers the ways in which ICT may be used in teaching and learning as well as for the identification and management of SEN. It provides a context and a framework for the chapters that follow.

In Chapter 2, Chris Stevens provides a historical perspective on ICT and SEN from the point of view of government initiatives in England and Wales. He argues that ICT can transform opportunities for independent learning and curriculum access for people with disabilities and he shows how UK government-sponsored research and development projects since the 1970s have contributed to current understandings about how to use technology to transform learning opportunities. Through this historical review, Stevens shows how local education authorities, schools and teachers each have an important role to play in ensuring that pupils with SEN have access to ICT.

Following Chris Stevens's review, Lesley Rahamin (Chapter 3) provides a historical perspective on her work as a teacher of pupils with SEN. She describes how technology has been used to improve access to the curriculum and participation in mainstream schools for pupils with SEN. Her chapter complements Stevens's history with case examples from many years' experience. Rahamin is realistic about the benefits and the *risks* of using ICT with pupils with SEN. She writes movingly about pupils with SEN in mainstream schools who found using ICT to be an isolating experience. This is an important point and one that we return to throughout the book. Although we argue that ICT has the potential for an 'equalizing effect' because it can be used to ameliorate the effects of certain impairments, we also argue that it must be used with care so that it does not inhibit but facilitates participation.

Chapter 4 is concerned with the use of computer-based assessment (CBA) to identify learning problems. This is an important issue for any teacher working with pupils with SEN, as the *Special Educational Needs Code of Practice* (Department for Education and Skills 2001) requires all teachers to participate in the identification and provision for pupils with SEN. In this chapter, Chris Singleton reviews the advantages of CBA and considers its relationship to conventional assessment. He provides illustrative case examples of how CBA has been used with individual pupils.

Moving on from assessment of individual learning problems, Chapter 5 provides a case study of a secondary school's experience of implementing an integrated learning system (ILS). Of interest here is how Ian Hedley contrasts the research on ILS with his experience. This provides an important reminder that there is often a gap between the vision of those who develop software and those who use it. As Hedley notes, the strength of an ILS is its 'ability' to individualize the material presented to the pupil, which implies that group work with an ILS would not be as effective as individual work. Yet Hedley found that pairs working collaboratively led to increased gains in reading and self-esteem.

In Chapter 6, Clive Lilley describes his experience as a headteacher of a special school for pupils with physical disabilities in developing a whole-school approach to ICT. Here ICT is presented as a means of achieving independence and control over one's environment. Technology is seen as a vehicle through which communication can occur. The expertise of staff at Lilley's school is so well developed that an outreach role has evolved where school staff are increasingly called upon to help colleagues in mainstream schools understand how ICT can support pupils with SEN. Like Lesley Rahamin in Chapter 3, Lilley is realistic about the benefits and the risks of using ICT with pupils with SEN. His list of 'frustrations and difficulties' offers important guidance for teachers planning to use ICT to support learning.

By sharing their research on virtual environments, Penny Standen and David Brown provide a detailed overview of an exciting innovation that has the potential to transform special education. Chapter 7 describes research and development work on the role of virtual environments as an educational tool for people with learning difficulties. Standen and Brown define virtual environments as 'computer-generated three-dimensional environments that respond in real time to the activity of the user'. They are considered particularly appropriate as a learning tool for pupils with intellectual disabilities because of the way in which the virtual environment can be 'scaffolded' to support the learner in mastering a complex task in a safe environment before real-world experience.

In Chapter 8, Allison Rees and Anna Williams shift our attention from teaching and learning with ICT to managing provision for SEN. The increased demands on teachers of pupils with special educational needs and on SEN coordinators have prompted the development of a number of software programs designed to help them manage the day-to-day responsibilities of providing for pupils with SEN. Rees and Williams present a case study of their own experience of using one of these packages. Like others in this volume who report on practical experience of implementing ICT, Rees and Williams experienced difficulties but draw upon the lessons they learned to offer guidelines for others interested in using such packages.

No book on ICT would be complete without a chapter on staff development and in Chapter 9 John Hegarty considers what is needed to help staff develop the skills necessary to use technology to support learners with SEN. This final chapter discusses ICT capability and the structures that are needed to support teachers to work creatively. In concluding this volume with a consideration of teacher development, we hope to underscore a theme running throughout the book: that ICT as a learning support for pupils with SEN depends on the skill of the teacher who plans and implements its many applications.

Technology can be used to overcome barriers to learning for *all* learners, but particularly those with disabilities, wherever that learning takes place. Although we use the word 'pupil' throughout the book for consistency, many of the applications described are of potential value to younger and older learners. The chapters in this book explore how ICT can be used to overcome barriers to learning and each chapter offers something to practitioners, whether they are teachers, teaching assistants, carers, tutors or specialists in mainstream or special settings.

References

Cuban, L. (2001) Why are most teachers infrequent and restrained users of computers in their classrooms?, in J. Woodward and L. Cuban (eds) *Technology, Curriculum and Professional Development: Adapting Schools to Meet the Needs of Students with Disabilities*. Thousand Oaks, CA: Corwin Press.

Department for Education and Skills (2001) *Special Educational Needs Code of Practice*. London: DfES.

1

USES OF TECHNOLOGY THAT SUPPORT PUPILS WITH SPECIAL EDUCATIONAL NEEDS

Lani Florian

Introduction

Much of the research on learning with technology has focused on different types of software programs. This research suggests that the effects are generally positive but that there are different effects for different types of programs and different groups of learners. In an extensive review, Lou *et al.* (2001) found that learner characteristics have an effect on learning with technology. These characteristics include computer experience, gender, ability and age. While teachers may not profess expertise in the technical aspects of ICT, they are expert in teaching and learning and, therefore, in a good position to determine how technology can best be used to help pupils learn and participate in classroom life.

This chapter provides an overview of some of the issues regarding teaching and learning with technology for learners with special educational needs (SEN), two areas of education that have undergone rapid development over recent decades. Investment in information and communications technology (ICT) and the development of policy and practice in meeting SEN have created unprecedented opportunity for the inclusion of *all* pupils in meaningful learning experiences wherever that learning takes place, be it in mainstream or special schools, college or work-based training. Indeed, it could be argued that the ubiquitous nature of technology in everyday life is such that much learning with ICT now takes place outside of formal educational environments. Cuban (2001) claims that the use of technology in the classroom is less frequent and more restrained than predicted. Yelland (2003) suggests that after-school environments may be more conducive for learning because children have access to more interesting software and are freer to explore and collaborate with others in solving problems. However, educational researchers are increasingly studying how children interact with technology in naturalistic settings and applying what they are learning to increase the power of technology as a pedagogical tool (National Research Council 2000; Pearson 2003).

It is important to consider what is meant by information and communications technology. Loveless and Ellis (2001: 2) point out that the term 'information and communications technology' describes a set of technologies that vary widely within and between subject areas. In England and Wales, ICT refers to a subject of the National Curriculum, but it is also used synonymously with terms like information technology, computer technology or simply technology. This, in turn, can include reference to hardware (the machinery), software (the kinds of programs that are available) or networks (communicating with others). Each of these aspects has implications for teaching and learning in general, and as the chapters in this book explore, there are specific implications for learners with various types of special educational needs. This chapter considers some of the issues in the field of special educational needs and looks at how information technology affects those issues.

Special educational needs

The term 'special educational needs' covers many kinds of difficulties in learning, and means different things to different people in different places. It covers an array of problems, from those related to particular impairments to those related to learning and behavioural difficulties experienced by some learners compared with other similar learners. In England and Wales, this is highlighted in the *Special Educational Needs Code of Practice*, which

> does not assume that there are hard and fast categories of special educational need. It recognises as LEAs [local education authorities] will recognise, that each child is unique and that the questions asked by LEAs should reflect the particular circumstances of that child. LEAs should recognise that there is a wide spectrum of special educational needs that are frequently inter-related, although there are also specific needs that usually relate directly to particular types of impairment . . . The areas of need are:

- communication and interaction
- cognition and learning
- behaviour, emotional and social development
- sensory and/or physical

(Department for Education and Skills 2001: §7:52, p. 85)

These areas of need may create barriers to learning unless adaptations are made. The process of making such adaptations is the essence of special education and it occurs in mainstream as well as special schools. Here it is necessary to distinguish between special education as segregation in a special school or class, and special education as the specialist teaching methods that have been developed to support the learning of pupils with SEN, particularly pupils with learning difficulties wherever they are placed.

In recent years, the concept of inclusion or inclusive education has emerged as a more equitable approach to meeting the needs of all learners and it has come to dominate special education practice throughout the world. As a model for meeting special educational needs, it requires the elimination of barriers to participation in education. There has been considerable debate about how this might best be achieved. Some argue that classroom teachers should take responsibility for providing the necessary support to help pupils overcome barriers to learning with specialist input as needed; others believe that learners who are experiencing difficulty should have direct access to specialists; still others argue that placement in specialist facilities is the best way to include some learners with special educational needs in education. To date, there has been no satisfactory resolution to this debate, although UK government policy has tended to favour models of inclusive education that promote a process of increasing participation and decreasing the exclusion of vulnerable students from the culture, curricula and communities of local schools (Booth *et al.* 2000).

Although the attempts to differentiate types of learners have been based on professional knowledge and good intention, the lines that are drawn to determine who gets special education and who does not could be argued to be arbitrary. One need only consider the range of definitions and eligibility criteria in different parts of the world to understand this point. But even within countries there is variability. In England and Wales, the variation between local education authorities in the number of children who get statements of SEN is five-fold (Audit Commission 2002). Thus eligibility for special education is not fixed but depends on many factors. However, regardless of the cause of a pupil's difficulty (whether it is because of an impairment, inappropriate teaching or a lack of opportunity to learn), there is always something the teacher can do to support the learner. And, as I argue in the following section, the use of ICT in responding to special educational needs opens new opportunities for participation and inclusion in the culture, curricula and communities of schools.

The potential of ICT for meeting SEN

It has been suggested that technology is a great equalizer, that for many people with disabilities technology can serve as a kind cognitive prosthesis to overcome or compensate for differences among learners. This idea has important implications for learners with disabilities and special educational needs because it suggests that technology can help create the conditions for equal opportunity to learn and equal access to the curriculum for all.

The appeal of technology as an equalizer for learners with special educational needs is borne out in the many materials that have been developed to address special educational needs. Professional magazines and trade shows offer a dazzling array of devices and programs covering all areas of the curriculum and all types of learning difficulties. For example, the official magazine of the UK's National Association for Special Educational Needs, *Special!*, contains an ICT guide as a regular feature. This feature explores a range of issues from reviews of programs to the skills that teaching assistants need to support learners. It covers all types of learning with technology for all kinds of learners. Similarly, the American *Journal of Special Education Technology* reports on research on the use of technology in the field of special educational needs.

The plethora of available information and the range of topics covered under the heading information and communications technology and SEN can be daunting. In the pressurized world of teaching, there is little opportunity to think critically about what is available or how it should be used. In a review of the instructional effectiveness of technology for pupils with SEN, Woodward *et al.* (2001) examined the research on software curriculum designed specifically for pupils with such needs. They identified a number of design variables thought to affect academic outcomes for pupils with SEN, such as the quantity and type of feedback, practice, strategy instruction, assessment and motivation. Woodward *et al.* found that there are no simple answers to the question of effectiveness: 'simply because a program or approach has been validated by research does not necessarily mean it will be used as intended in practice' (p. 21).

Means (1994) argues that the application of ICT, the ways in which teachers use it, must start with the teacher and the kind of learning they want to foster. She categorizes ICT by the ways in which it is used in teaching. From her perspective, ICT can be used to tutor or to explore; it can be applied as a tool and it can be used to communicate. In the field of special education, ICT is also used for assessment and management purposes. The sections below consider these six uses of ICT and their applications to learners with special educational needs.

Used to tutor

Tutor programs represent a longstanding type of teaching with technology. The earliest programs were intended to help teachers individualize learning and learners to work at their own pace. Known as computer-assisted instruction (CAI), many software programs for pupils with and without SEN were developed and commercially published. These programs had a particular appeal to teachers of pupils with SEN because they offered a way of addressing what Woodward and Rieth (1997: 507) called 'one of the field's most perplexing logistical and pedagogical dilemmas'; that is, how to individualize teaching to meet the particular needs of pupils who are experiencing difficulties in learning. And as Woodward and Rieth point out, this is, after all, what special needs education is all about.

Most early CAI programs were based on a behavioural theory of learning. Typically, learners worked individually at a computer on tasks that tended to emphasize drill and practice, or the reinforcement of previously taught skills. Many programs may have been delivered via computer software but, in terms of their design and content, they were no different than conventional materials for drill and practice. In other words, the medium (use of microcomputer as opposed to a workbook) was different but the content (basic skills) and the purpose (drill and practice) were the same as in conventional teaching.

The impracticality of one-to-one work at computer stations, changing views of teaching and learning, and advances in technology led to the development of more sophisticated and complex tutor programs as well as group approaches to learning with technology. Researchers began to exploit the potential of ICT by incorporating more pedagogical principles into software design, notably in the use of feedback. In an extensive review of the literature on technology research in special education, Woodward and Rieth (1997) reported mixed results for the use of computer programs to generate feedback to pupils with SEN. They concluded that, on its own, CAI was insufficient for teaching pupils with SEN.

However, individualized learning programs retain their appeal, particularly as a supplementary support for learners with special educational needs. Indeed, many schools have looked keenly towards the highly sophisticated 'integrated learning systems' (see Chapter 5), which incorporate high levels of computer management to individualize learning. More recent developments in designing CAI for pupils with SEN have incorporated strategy instruction techniques in an attempt to explicitly teach the problem-solving strategies involved in completing a task. Gunter *et al.* describe how they used Microsoft Excel to teach pupils with specific learning difficulties to monitor their academic performance:

> Having [pupils with specific learning difficulties] self-evaluate their social and academic performance is a strategy with proven benefits. Adding the

component of self-graphing seems to further enhance the effectiveness. Finally, with improved, user-friendly technology and software packages, [pupils] can easily learn to record and graph high quality representations of their work performance. Having [pupils] involved with the production of the graphic display of their performance data not only has potential benefits for [pupils with SEN] but simultaneously enhances teachers' efficient use of time.

(Gunter *et al.* 2002: 33)

In this example, Gunter *et al.* applied the pedagogical principles of strategy instruction – in this case, self-monitoring – in the design of a CAI application using commonly available software.

An important issue in the use of tutor programs with pupils with SEN is the extent to which they are used to include or exclude learners from participation in group activities. A balance needs to be struck between the benefit of working individually at one's own pace and the isolation that some learners experience when such an emphasis precludes participation in group activities. Consideration needs to be given to how the program *facilitates* participation.

Used to explore

Over time, as technology has become more powerful and accessible, exploratory learning environments have been developed. Though they have not replaced tutor programs, they are in contrast to them. Whereas tutor programs are about teaching, exploratory learning environments allow pupils to interact with the material and have more control over their learning. Exploratory environments represent an increasingly popular contemporary use of technology in education. They emphasize exploration as opposed to drill and practice or the reinforcement of skills and knowledge. They are based on constructivist rather than the behavioural views of learning. The idea is to promote authentic learning with an emphasis on assisting learners to collaboratively construct knowledge (Reed and McNergney 2000). Exploratory learning environments include simulations and virtual environments such as those described in Chapter 8, as well as framework programs (also called 'content-free' programs).

Such approaches to the use of technology are touted as tools that enable teachers and pupils to become co-learners who collaboratively construct knowledge (Reed and McNergney 2000). For example, framework programs enable teachers and learners to construct personalized cause-and-effect activities. Using a digital camera, one can record a trip or experience for later review. The technology permits the use of real-world examples to 'learn by doing'.

Stanford and Siders (2001) developed an e-mail pen friend correspondence project. They were interested in improving the writing skills of pupils with specific learning difficulties and were influenced by other research that showed a positive effect for the use of word processing on the writing skills of such pupils. They found a significant effect in favour of e-mail pen friends compared with conventional pen friends and a control group who wrote to imaginary pen friends and received no replies to their letters. Stanford and Siders suggested that while any kind of pen friend offers pupils a genuine and authentic experience, email pen friends receive instant feedback. If a pupil with SEN is paired with a model e-pal – for example, someone with superior writing skills – the model e-pal will provide guidance to the pupil with SEN.

Other pupils with SEN have more severe learning difficulties and, because of the nature of their impairments and/or the amount of support they require, have fewer opportunities to explore and control their environment. For these pupils, exploratory environments such as simulations and virtual environments can offer opportunities for learning that might otherwise not be available. Pupils are presented with an authentic and challenging task and they control the activity. As Means has observed:

> Given complex tasks, students take a more active part in defining their own learning goals and regulating their own learning. They explore ideas and bodies of knowledge, not in order to repeat back verbal formulations on demand but to understand phenomena and find information they need for their project work. When students work on complex tasks, their work will often cross over the borders of academic disciplines, just as real world problems often demand the application of several kinds of expertise. In this *multi-disciplinary context*, instruction becomes *interactive*. The nature of the information and the support provided for students will change as the problems they work on change and evolve over time.
>
> (Means 1994: 6–7; emphasis in the original)

The use of exploratory environments often offers the opportunity to personalize material by using sounds and pictures that are familiar to the learner. When these options are available, it is important to consider the assumptions that one is making about the learner when devising such environments. It is worth asking whether the learner has been involved in the construction of the material and, if so, how?

The Internet offers yet another example of how ICT can be used to explore. The opportunities to do so are limitless, since information can be sent and explored in many mediums (text, pictures or sound). Banes and Walter (2002: 25) offer useful guidelines for using the Internet as an exploratory environment for pupils with SEN in schools. Lessons using the Internet should:

- Be incorporated into the total communication policy at the school. This includes the use of speech, signing, rebus symbols, written words and voice output communication aids.
- Be rooted in the concrete experiences of pupils.
- Enable pupils access to other individuals and groups through e-mail and special interest groups.
- Promote individual educational aims in cross-curricula areas.
- Promote access to English (speaking and listening, writing, reading) within the curriculum.
- Support the application of the National Curriculum with pupils in various curriculum areas.
- Promote communication with individuals and groups outside school.
- Develop writing and communication skills, by following a process of plan–draft–revise–proof read–present and by making judgements about tone, style, format and choice of vocabulary as appropriate to the intended audience.

Applied as tools

The third type of learning with ICT is about the skills (and for some pupils with SEN, the adaptations) involved in using the tools of technology, such as word-processing programs, spreadsheets and hand-held computers; in other words, the tools found in non-educational environments such as the home or workplace. Indeed, acquiring technical skills is not only pre-requisite to the other types of learning with technology, but is increasingly essential for life beyond school.

The use of hand-held computers provides a good example of how a new technology can affect classroom participation. Bauer and Ulrich (2002) found that the use of hand-held computers helped pupils with SEN to stay organized. Pupils with SEN in their study of the use of hand-held computers in Year 6 said that the computers reduced anxiety about knowing what they needed to do or losing papers. This was attributed to the portability of the technology. Bauer and Ulrich also suggest that hand-held computers offer social support, as pupils can share programs with each other and send information to friends.

For some learners with special educational need, skill is not only about the technical aspects of learning how to use hardware and software, but also about using the adaptations that are made to enable the learner to exercise the skill. Many assistive devices are available to overcome the barriers to learning posed by physical and sensory impairments. Access devices range from simple switches and touch screens to specialist keyboards and voice-activated software. But they are not in themselves a panacea: significant skill is needed to operate them successfully.

Paveley (2002) notes that, although the World Wide Web would appear to be an ideal medium for teaching and learning for pupils with SEN, much of it is not accessible. She describes a range of practical ways that pupils with learning difficulties can be supported in accessing the Web. For example, she describes a project using graphics from pupils' favourite websites to create links to websites on overlay keyboards. This was developed as an alternative for pupils who were unable to access Bookmarks or a Favourites list. For switch users, for whom the Web can pose significant difficulties, Banes and Walter (2002) provide detailed information on the use of switches as adaptive devices for accessing the Web.

If children are to use ICT as a tool successfully, a comprehensive assessment of their strengths and needs is vital. Hardy (2000) suggests that such an assessment should include information on the following:

- the learner, including ability across the curriculum, current ICT skills and a rationale for why ICT provision would be helpful;
- support available for the pupil;
- information about the school;
- an evaluation including the goals set and a date for review; and
- financial considerations.

Hardy argues that access to the curriculum should drive ICT assessment.

Information and communications technology is both a means and an end. In Hardy's (2000) assessment framework, ICT is considered as a means to accessing the curriculum. When it is being taught as a subject of the curriculum, one must think about assessment in terms of the end product or aim of the curriculum – in this case, computer literacy. Assessment of computer literacy focuses on the proficiency and experience of specific ICT skills and this is where consideration must be given to the accommodations that would enable the learner to overcome barriers to participation in ICT as a subject of the curriculum.

Used to communicate

There are many assistive technology devices available to help pupils communicate. These include electronic language boards, voice synthesizers and voice recognition software. Many of the symbol communication systems used by some pupils with SEN are supported by software programs to enable pupils, for example, to write and e-mail.

Communication media exploit networks that allow groups of learners to communicate (Lou *et al.* 2001). Bulletin boards, e-mail and chat rooms are common examples of how networks can be used. Like the other types of learning with technology, these applications of network technology are multi-faceted. They can have a particularly 'equalizing effect' because participants choose what to disclose about themselves. Disability or special educational need is not a defining characteristic of the participant, nor is it necessarily a barrier to participation.

Networked communication is also being promoted as a means of facilitating participation in the mainstream virtual world inhabited both by people with and without disabilities. A good example is e-Buddies (www.ebuddies.org), an e-mail 'pen friend' program. This project is designed to support people with special educational needs to find and make friends on the Internet. Here the 'equalizing effect' has to do with targeting a particular group of people as a means of facilitating participation. Participation can be helped by specialist adaptations – for example, the use of symbols in e-mail (Banes and Walter 2002).

There has been very little research on how networked communication might help pupils with SEN. Bauer and Ulrich (2002) reported the use of hand-held computers to engender social support for pupils with special educational needs though they cautioned that the teacher must manage their use. Abbott (2002) also considers the management difficulties in using technology for communication. The unmoderated and uncensored nature of on-line chat, for example, may render it inappropriate for educational purposes. Yet the equalizing effect it offers some pupils with SEN clearly makes it a valuable educational resource. Abbott recommends careful planning before embarking on communication projects. Projects should involve people who know each other (for example, colleagues from other schools) and the use of filtering software on the school network.

Means (1994: 13) reminds us that the tools and communication devices of technology do not have value in and of themselves. Rather, their 'instructional value lies in the educational activity that uses the tools and communication devices, an activity that must be planned by the teacher'.

Used for assessment purposes

Teachers working with pupils who experience difficulties in learning are often called upon to play a role in assessing the nature of the child's learning difficulty. The *Special Educational Needs Code of Practice* (Department for Education and Skills 2001) stipulates that ongoing observation and assessment should be undertaken in the identification of pupils with SEN. Formative assessment procedures are not required; instead, schools are left to decide what procedures they should adopt for meeting the needs of all children. Although care must be taken to distinguish between statutory assessments, which lead to statements of special educational need, and formative assessments, which assist in pinpointing the specific difficulty a pupil may be experiencing in learning, there has been a great deal of research interest in the use of technology to assist in the diagnosis of learning difficulties.

Woodward and Rieth (1997) argue that 'technology has come to be seen as a vehicle for orchestrating higher-quality assessment and reducing the amount of time humans manage the assessment process' (p. 517).

Computer programs that offer curriculum-based assessment (CBA) provide a means for systematic and cost-effective assessment, as they replace the labour-intensive procedures normally undertaken by teaching staff. These programs are often, but not exclusively, based on behavioural views of learning, although some applications are based on dynamic assessment techniques, which alert pupils to different types of errors, as well as those that use self-monitoring (for example, Gunter et al. 2002, described above), which encourages pupils to monitor their own progress.

Although they are seen as teacher-friendly tools that are intended to help teachers work more efficiently, computer-based assessment systems can offer more than a means of recording and summarizing data. As Woodward and Rieth (1997) point out, recent versions of computer-based assessment systems incorporate expert systems that enable teachers to be provided with suggestions for intervention for specific learning or behavioural difficulties. This is especially important, as teachers often need support in generating new strategies when what they have tried does not work. In another review, Woodward et al. (2001) hailed the application of expert systems to assessment as one of the more advanced efforts to apply 'state-of-the-art' technologies to special education problems.

Used as a management tool

In addition to assessing learning difficulties, teachers of pupils with SEN are required to develop individual education plans (IEPs) designed to address identified learning difficulties. They may also be called upon to participate in the statutory assessment process prior to issuing a statement of special educational need. Like all teachers, they are required to set targets and monitor pupil progress; however, for those pupils with SEN who work below level 1 of the National Curriculum, alternative arrangements for monitoring progress are required.

As a result of the increased demands on teachers of pupils with SEN and special educational needs coordinators (SENCOs), a number of software programs designed to help them manage the day-to-day responsibilities of providing for pupils with SEN have been developed. The range of learning difficulties covered by the umbrella term SEN is vast and no one teacher will know about all the potential difficulties individual pupils may experience. This partly explains the appeal of expert systems in the development of special needs diagnostic software. An expert system could be devised to have more information than an individual teacher could retain and, therefore, teachers could use them to help generate teaching solutions to individual learning problems.

The Internet is an increasingly popular management tool for SEN professionals for the same reason. Male and Gotthoffer (1999) have developed a workbook for teachers to guide them through the Internet to special education resources. In addition to websites that contain information on a topic, there are many special education discussion group lists to which one can subscribe. The British Educational and Communications Technology Agency, Becta, described in Chapter 2, hosts several of these, including the popular SENCO-FORUM for special educational needs coordinators and SENIT for educationalists interested specifically in ICT. Such lists (see, for example, Majordomo@ngfl.gov.uk) create a forum for people to share common interests and problems, share expertise and solve problems.

More recently, researchers have begun to use the Internet to publish information. Dee *et al.* (2002) developed web-based curriculum guidance to support the transition of pupils with learning difficulties from school to adult life (http://www.qca.org.uk/ca/inclusion/p16_ld/index.asp). This project, commissioned in England by the Qualifications and Curriculum Authority (QCA), provides guidance to practitioners working in a range of post-school settings, including schools, colleges and work-based training. Web-based materials have the advantage of hyperlinks that enable users to move around the site by clicking the various hyperlinks. In this way, the user can make his or her own connections between the components. However, as Dee and her colleagues point out, little is known about how teachers and other training personnel use web-based materials. They note the need for research into precisely how practitioners interact with web-based materials to inform the design of future materials.

Conclusions

The types of learning with, and uses of, information and communications technology discussed above are not finite or fixed categories. Indeed, there are other ways of organizing a discussion around the aspects and varieties of ICT. In addition, one could argue that there is some overlap between the categories; for example, software programs with design characteristics that would enable them to be used as tutor *or* exploratory programs, or as tutor *and* diagnostic programs. The use of Means's four types of learning with technology plus assessment and management purposes was used simply as an organizational device within which broad issues of ICT and SEN might be considered.

Providing access to technology to schools is not the same as making sure every learner has access. Access might require adaptations to accommodate different learners. In addition, these adaptations might involve one or more of the types of learning with technology discussed above. Loveless and Ellis (2001) were right to point out that ICT is not a single entity but refers to a set of technologies. Moreover, ICT offers distinct opportunities and challenges to learners with disabilities and special educational needs. The challenges include the adaptations that may have to be made for learners to acquire or use the tools of technology. The opportunities lie in the way that technology can then be used to ameliorate the effects of what would otherwise create a barrier to learning or participation in an interactive activity.

References

Abbott, C. (2002) Making communication special, in C. Abbott (ed.) *Special Educational Needs and the Internet: Issues for the Inclusive Classroom*. London: Routledge/Falmer.

Audit Commission (2002) *Statutory Assessment and Statements of Special Educational Needs: In Need of Review?* London: Audit Commissioner.

Banes, D. and Walter, R. (2002) *Internet for All*. London: David Fulton.

Bauer, A.M. and Ulrich, M.E. (2002) 'I've got a palm in my pocket': using handheld computers in an inclusive classroom, *Teaching Exceptional Children*, 35(2): 18–22.

Booth, T., Ainscow, M., Black-Hawkins, K., Vaughan, M. and Shaw, L. (2000) *Index for Inclusion: Developing, Learning and Participation in Schools*. Bristol: CSIE.

Cuban, L. (2001) Why are most teachers infrequent and restrained users of computers in their classrooms?, in J. Woodward and L. Cuban (eds) *Technology, Curriculum and Professional Development: Adapting Schools to Meet the Needs of Students with Disabilities*. Thousand Oaks, CA: Corwin Press.

Dee, L., Florian, L., Porter, J. and Robertson, C. (2002) Developing curriculum guidance for person-centred transitions. Paper presented to the European Educational Research Association Conference on Educational Research, Lisbon, September.

Department for Education and Skills (2001) *Special Educational Needs Code of Practice*. London: DfES.

Gunter, P.L., Miller, K.A., Venn, M.L., Thomas, K. and House, S. (2002) Self-graphing to success: computerized data management, *Teaching Exceptional Children*, 35(2): 30–4.

Hardy, C. (2000) *Information and Communications Technology for All*. London: David Fulton.

Lou, Y., Abrami, P.C. and d'Apollonia, S. (2001) Small group and individual learning with technology: a meta-analysis, *Review of Educational Research*, 71(3): 449–521.

Loveless, A. and Ellis, V. (2001) *ICT, Pedagogy and the Curriculum: Subject to Change*. London: Routledge/Falmer.

Male, M. and Gotthoffer, D. (1999) *Quick Guide to the Internet for Special Education*. Boston, MA: Allyn & Bacon.

Means, B. (ed.) (1994) *Technology and Education Reform: The Reality Behind the Promise*. San Francisco, CA: Josssey-Bass.

National Research Council (2000) *How People Learn: Brain, Mind, Experience and School*. Washington, DC: National Research Council.

Paveley, S. (2002) Inclusion and the Web: strategies to improve access, in C. Abbott (ed.) *Special Educational Needs and the Internet: Issues for the Inclusive Classroom*. London: Routledge/Falmer.

Pearson, M. (2003) Online searching as apprenticeship: young people and web search strategies, in G. Marshall and Y. Katz (eds) *Learning in School, Home and Community: ICT for Early and Elementary Education*. London: Kluwer Academic.

Reed, D.S. and McNergney, R.F. (2000) *Evaluating Technology-based Curriculum Materials*. ERIC Digest EDO-SP-2000–5. Washington, DC: ERIC Clearinghouse on Teaching and Teacher Education.

Stanford, P. and Siders, J.A. (2001) E-pal writing! *Teaching Exceptional Children*, 34(2): 21–4.

Woodward, J. and Rieth, H. (1997) A historical review of technology research in special education, *Review of Educational Research*, 67(4): 503–36.

Woodward, J., Gallagher, D. and Rieth, H. (2001) The instructional effectiveness of technology for students with disabilities, in J. Woodward and L. Cuban (eds) *Technology, Curriculum and Professional Development: Adapting Schools to Meet the Needs of Students with Disabilities*. Thousand Oaks, CA: Corwin Press.

Yelland, N. (2003) Learning in school and out: formal and informal experiences with computer games in mathematical contexts, in G. Marshall and Y. Katz (eds) *Learning in School, Home and Community: ICT for Early and Elementary Education*. London: Kluwer Academic.

2

INFORMATION AND COMMUNICATIONS TECHNOLOGY, SPECIAL EDUCATIONAL NEEDS AND SCHOOLS: A HISTORICAL PERSPECTIVE OF UK GOVERNMENT INITIATIVES

Chris Stevens

The benefits of using technology to help people with learning difficulties and disabilities have been acknowledged for centuries. If you go into the Church near the Abbey in the Yorkshire town of Whitby, you will see around the pulpit a range of ear trumpets. These were placed there during the nineteenth century to enable the then Rector's wife, who was deaf, hear the Sunday sermon. Without that technology, someone in the congregation may have been excluded from worship.

The inventive use of supportive equipment has been a key consideration for those caring for and working with people with disabilities. At times, it has led to the creative application of technology intended for another purpose. For example, in 1821 a soldier named Charles Barber visited a school for the blind. He brought with him a system he had invented called 'night writing'. 'Night writing' had originally been designed so soldiers could pass instructions along trenches at night without having to talk and give their positions away. It consisted of twelve raised dots that could be combined to represent different sounds.

Unfortunately, it proved to be too complex for soldiers to master and was therefore rejected by the Army. The young Louis Braille quickly realized how useful this system of raised dots could be for blind people and the rest is history.

As technologies have developed, the need to harness the opportunities they offer for supporting and enhancing the life of people with disabilities has become increasingly important. This is especially true in the use of information and communications technology (ICT) in teaching and learning. However, it would be wrong to assume that this view has always been self-evident to all. The realization that using ICT can transform people's opportunities to access the curriculum through independent learning is only now becoming widely acknowledged.

This chapter reviews the UK government's developing interest in the use of ICT since the 1970s, with particular reference to special educational needs (SEN). Information and communications technology can be used to support these pupils by providing:

- physical access to learning, as in the case of pupils' use of switches to operate computers where they are physically unable to use a traditional keyboard;
- cognitive access through a multimedia approach that does not rely only on the written word to offer information but can enhance this by using sound and visual reinforcement;
- support for learning through on-line assessment opportunities and linking this to appropriate materials which offer opportunities for pupils to make progress at an appropriate rate.

The early years

During the 1970s, educators were becoming increasingly convinced that computers had the potential for supporting learners in formal education, even though the equipment available at the time was costly and not user-friendly. In 1970, the British Computer Society set up a schools' committee. Although the focus for discussion in this group was why children should learn about computers rather than how they could be useful in the curriculum, it did begin a debate that was to continue for the rest of the century.

The first sign of government recognition of the potential of information technology (IT), as it was then known, within education more broadly came in 1973 with the establishment of the National Development Programme for Computer Assisted Learning. This was a 4-year programme with a budget of little more than £2 million. The programme lasted for 5 years and supported 35 projects in schools and other educational establishments investigating the ways in which technology could be used as a medium for teaching and learning and to support the management of education.

Inevitably, these early years and the view of what schools could real-istically do using computers were limited by the technology available. Before the advent of microcomputers in the mid-1970s, software generally was becoming available for sale. However, mainframe computers provided no standards in this area at the time. Dissemination of what was available was not widespread, and while there were attempts to standardize, there was insufficient hardware around to make software sales viable.

The question at the time was: 'Could these machines support teaching and learning and if so how?' Although there were champions for the use of IT, they still had much convincing to do. Government, while open to persuasion in the field, were not about to expend large amounts of funds to promote practice in the field without more evidence of its efficacy.

If anything, the development of IT in education was still based on soci-ety's needs and ambitions. It was a concern that, despite the number of advertisements for jobs involving the use of computers, not enough was being done in schools to prepare young people to meet these challenges. Then, in 1979 the BBC broadcast its first popular programme about com-puting, 'Now the chips are down'. It was rumoured that this was watched by the then Prime Minister, Jim Callaghan, who was said to have recog-nized the potential of IT in education. Although his government fell from power that year, the seed was sown and the 1980s were to be the decade when investigation of what technology had to offer developed into more focused research, dissemination of good practice and training.

The 1980s: a decade of discovery

In many ways, the 1980s were the start of a roller coaster of change in the use of IT in education. Schools climbed on the roller coaster and are still riding it today. Teachers who were trained in an era before the role of IT was fully considered have had to come to terms not only with the technology's enormous potential, but also with the speed at which it is developing.

In 1980, the new Conservative government established the national Microelectronics Education Programme. The aim of this programme was to help local education authorities (LEAs) to set up support services for schools. This initiative was to be seminal in developing understanding of the ways in which pupils with learning difficulties and disabilities could benefit from the use of IT. In 1982, four special education micro-electronic resource centres (SEMERCs) were established through this programme. The initial remit of these centres was to provide a focus for developments, software, peripherals, expertise and training to support the needs of pupils with moderate learning difficulties. This remit was to grow, change and broaden as a result of subsequent initiatives, but the needs of these learn-ers were to provide an important focus for special needs and ICT.

The special education micro-electronic resource centres also produced briefing sheets. These were short, finely focused information pamphlets describing the function of the regional centres and providing suggestions on software which addressed areas such as the development of writing, oral language and mathematics. At the time, teachers in almost all special schools became aware of the centres and many obtained software information from them or attended SEMERC courses. Materials developed by the resource centres were released in 'free copiable' form. They were adaptable and flexible to meet the needs of experienced users of IT as well as novices as they planned their teaching and learning.

Courses devised for local education authority IT/SEN coordinators were a popular aspect of the work of the special education micro-electronic resource centres and were often attended by staff from all LEAs in the region. The courses had clearly stated aims and enabled attendees to review new materials, draft policy documents and guidelines, prepare INSET resources and exemplar activities for pupils using the new software.

The main overall achievements of the Microelectronics Education Programme were to heighten public awareness of the role of information technology in education, to establish networks of expertise in educational use of IT and to produce a variety of curriculum resources and training materials, including materials for use with pupils who had SEN. By 1986, most LEAs had established support and advisory services and many had advisers with a specialism in IT and SEN. The agenda was moving forward and gained a momentum that appeared to be unstoppable.

In July 1985, the Secretary of State for Education, Sir Keith Joseph, announced his intention to develop further the work of the Microelectronics Education Programme by establishing the Microelectronics Education Support Unit with an initial grant of £2.8 million and a brief to cover England, Wales, Scotland and Northern Ireland. Its remit was

> to provide support to local authorities in a number of clearly defined areas, namely the provision of a central information service; the training of trainers; and the development of relevant curricular materials for use in schools. The Government will also support, through the new Unit and the existing network for special education, the further development of microelectronics in this field.
>
> (Department of Education and Science 1990: 4)

In July 1987, the Department of Education and Science announced the IT in Schools Initiative (MESU 1987). In particular, this initiative enabled LEAs to strengthen or establish teams of advisory teachers for IT. These teams were appointed in equal proportions from primary and secondary sectors, but fewer than 10 per cent possessed expertise in SEN.

The initiative provided policy, structure, some physical resources and an element of professional support for teachers. The Microelectronics Education Support Unit was asked to provide curriculum and INSET materials and to coordinate and participate in the national programme of training for more than 600 advisory teachers from widely differing backgrounds and expertise, funded through the grants. The courses had to address the professional skills needed for advisory work and, in a second phase, to focus on particular subjects or aspects of the curriculum, particularly teachers of pupils with SEN.

The Microelectronics Education Support Unit operated an efficient and professionally run information service on ICT and teaching and learning. A special needs software centre was established on the SEMERC site in Manchester with a remit to develop software and associated materials for children with SEN. It funded several projects that effectively disseminated good practice and useful materials. Examples of this include their publications on INSET resources for primary mathematics, Pipistrel software (MESU 1988), a simulation programme and Rainbow (Coupland *et al.* 1988), which provided resources to support teachers of pupils transferring from primary to secondary schools. The Microelectronics Education Support Unit (MESU) also raised the profile of the educational use of IT through its own activities and publications and through the national and educational media. This promotion and persuasion role was to continue in the work of its successor organizations.

In addition to the work outlined above, twelve of the MESU staff were based at the Unit's four SEMERCs, each with a senior project leader in charge and reporting to a curriculum director in MESU.

When central funding for SEMERCs was removed in April 1989, many LEAs were slow to complete preparations for continuing their work. As late as January of that year, only a small minority of authorities, mainly in the north-west, had established cooperative arrangements to continue professional and technical support services for their schools. In most areas, advisers for SEN still had to negotiate and finalize contracts to replace the support functions on which many of their schools and SEN advisory teachers had come to rely. In the subsequent decade, the good work of the SEMERCs was to some extent lost in some of the areas previously served by the centres, and this led to comments like those of Her Majesty's Inspectorate, which found that

the impact of the SEMERCs and the software centres on classroom practice was generally dependent on the quality of LEA support for IT in schools with SEN. While their materials were found in most special schools, the extent of development of good practice and active use of IT in classrooms remained highly variable and not widespread.

(Department of Education and Science 1990: 3)

Closely associated with the SEMERCs were the Aids to Communication in Education Centres (ACE), which began operation in 1984. The Centres began after a project in an Oxfordshire school, originally funded by the Nuffield Foundation to develop content-free software for children with complex needs, was taken over and continued by the Department of Education and Science. This Centre assessed individual pupils requiring IT aids and provided support for professionals working with these children. It was felt that a similar centre was needed in the north of England and Oldham Metropolitan Borough Council agreed to share the funding with the Microelectronics Education Support Unit. Therapists were originally funded by charities but are now supported by the Department for Education and Skills.

Referrals for assessment came from a range of sources, including LEAs, schools and parents. Additionally, the ACE Centre Oxford has maintained a high profile in research and development. Today, both Centres continue to be active in training, publications and lobbying on issues related to children with communication difficulties.

The late 1980s

In the area of SEN, the 1980s saw a growing realization that technology not only had the potential for supporting learning, but for some learners it provided the *only* means of accessing the curriculum. Information technology was a lifeline that enabled them to become independent learners and participants in society. For many, IT made it possible to demonstrate achievements that previously would have been unthinkable. The place IT has in empowering those with learning difficulties and disabilities became increasingly well understood during the 1980s. Measures were taken not only to capture that knowledge and understanding, but also to disseminate it to a wide range of teachers across the educational spectrum.

Large amounts of government money were invested in research, development and dissemination projects. Partnerships were formed between central and local government, and schools were often beacons of good practice, which exemplified what could be done with the resources, the will and the determination of staff. However, at the end of the decade there was still much to be done. While there were pockets of very good practice, many teachers were still neither confident nor competent in using technology in the curriculum. Few denied its value but its use was often bolted on to what was still seen as the main pedagogical approaches. The 1990s had to change that view and make technology a part of the teacher's tool kit to be brought out and used in their planning and teaching in a fully integrated way.

In 1990, the ACE Centres were involved in a Department of Education and Science initiative to provide technological aids that helped pupils who had difficulty with verbal communication. From 1992 to 1995, they were instrumental in the establishment of a Joint Working Party with the Departments of Health and Education looking at the provision of communication aids for children. The group developed a number of important initiatives that made significant contributions to the promotion of effective use of technology with pupils who had communication difficulties. Joint funding by some LEAs and health authorities became available to purchase expensive communication aids, training for staff using and assessing pupils was provided by the ACE Centres and publications were financed that highlighted good practice in the multidisciplinary approach to identifying and meeting pupils' technology needs. These were targeted at practitioners, purchasers and providers. Embedding the use of technology was very much the name of the game.

At the end of the decade, financial restraint both locally and nationally meant innovation in education was under threat. The 1990s were likely to be a time of consolidation, reflection and budgetary cutbacks. At least in the first part of the decade, this created an environment in which spending on expensive resources and training to use ICT in schools short of money was seen as a luxury rather than a necessity.

However, the 1990s were to be a decade of great developments. What was it that happened to make this possible?

The 1990s

The IT in Schools Initiative lasted until 1993 and channelled £90 million into support and training for schools' use of ICT. Education support grants were superseded by grants for educational support and training (GEST). Also at this time, the Microelectronics Education Support Unit and the Council for Educational Technology amalgamated to form the National Council for Educational Technology, with a remit to carry on training, especially in the area of supporting pupils with learning difficulties and disabilities.

Alongside developments in ICT, new priorities were about to hit schools with a vengeance. In 1988, the Education Reform Act gave schools increased independence from LEAs, a trend that was to continue through the 1990s. At the same time, the Act put in motion the development of a National Curriculum. This was to consume the energies of most teachers in maintained schools throughout the first half of the 1990s. As in so many other walks of life people set priorities, and there is little doubt that when the National Curriculum Orders became set in law teachers spent enormous amounts of time coming to grips with their requirements. Many other areas of innovation moved down their priority list. It was certainly the case in the school where I was headteacher, a school for pupils with severe and profound and multiple learning difficulties. Staff development and training was focused on producing schemes of work that fitted in with the new National Curriculum requirements but still met the individual needs of pupils.

Many hoped that IT would be placed at the centre of the new curriculum and that this would drive the agenda forward with a clear lead on both developing pupils' IT capabilities and ensuring that IT would be used as one means of teaching across all subjects. In the event, this did not happen. Information technology was not designated a 'core subject'; indeed, it did not even have its own separate National Curriculum Order and it shared a ring binder with design and technology. In terms of using IT to support teaching across all National Curriculum subjects, this was not clearly or consistently defined. As Bill Tagg (1995) said in an article in *Computer Education*, 'the [subject] working groups which were set up worked independently. If they happened to have anyone who was IT orientated, that was lucky so that for many subjects the references to IT made strange reading' (p. 81). Advice on the development of IT as a way to support learning was left to a range of non-statutory guidance and support produced by organizations such as the National Curriculum Council and the National Council for Educational Technology.

It was not until the limitations of the original National Curriculum Orders became clear that the government embarked on a revision of the National Curriculum in 1994. Gillian Shepherd, the then Secretary of State, gave the job to Sir Ron Dearing, who had a clear brief to slim down the content of the new subject Orders and also, among other things, to review the place of IT in the overall curriculum structure. The outcome of this review achieved three important results as far as IT was concerned. For the first time a separate Order for IT was created, giving recognition to programmes of study as the content of the subject in its own right (even though unexpanded from the original Orders). Information technology carried a statutory requirement to be taught at all key stages. Finally, in the common requirements for all National Curriculum subjects, except physical education, IT was to be used in teaching the subject 'where appropriate'. Pupils for the first time had a statutory right to be taught to develop their IT capability and to harness the power of technology across all other subjects.

The government also realized that to advance the use of technology in education it was necessary to build an IT infrastructure in schools and LEAs to turn the rhetoric into reality. The early part of the 1990s saw the launch of a range of initiatives designed to place large amounts of hardware and software into schools. In 1992, £4 million was made available under GEST funding through the CD-ROM in Secondary Schools scheme, which was extended to primary schools, with a further £4.5 million in 1994 and £5 million in 1995. These schemes were expected to equip all secondary and 2800 primary schools with at least one multimedia computer and a selection of CD-ROM titles.

At the same time, the power of newer technologies to help both pupils and teachers was becoming evident. In 1995, research was commissioned by the Department for Education and Employment and 70 industrial sponsors through the Education Department's Superhighways Initiative. This investigated the use of intermediate and broadband technologies across the education system and fed into the major development of the 1990s, the National Grid for Learning. Teachers' use of technology to support their work was not ignored and between 1996 and 1997 over 2650 teachers, including teachers in special schools, were equipped with portable computers with Internet access through the Multimedia Portables for Teachers schemes run by the National Council for Educational Technology.

Activity in the mid-1990s aimed at getting hardware into schools, developing teaching and learning materials with publishers and increasing the confidence and competence of teachers in their use of ICT. However, there did not appear to be a clear underpinning rationale and it was often money left in departmental budgets at year-end rather than that made available to fund year-on-year expenditure that was financing developments. What was lacking was a comprehensive overall plan for the way forward that had been thought through and costed.

The Labour Party in opposition realized this and commissioned an inquiry into ICT in UK schools. This enquiry was led by Sir Dennis Stevenson and reported in March 1997 with an allied and more technical report by McKinsey and Co. (1997) being published at the same time. They reported that in spite of the growing number of initiatives, the 'state of ICT in our schools is primitive and not improving' (Stevenson 1997: 6). Much hardware was old and out of date and the computer to pupil ratio was up to 1 to 30 in many schools. Very little software was related to the curriculum, and the way ICT was being used varied greatly. The report recommended that there was a 'national priority to increase the use of ICT in our schools' and that central government 'must make the act of faith and encourage the education sector to start using technology rather than talking about it!' (Stevenson 1997: 6).

The Stevenson Report (1997: 7–9) advocated a 5–10 year strategy, consistently maintained, to ensure the use of technology becomes fundamental to teaching and learning in this country. It recommended a range of actions, including:

1. The government should announce its intention of addressing the use of ICT in schools as top priority with ministerial responsibility for driving policies.
2. An initiative for both teachers in training and in schools to learn how ICT can be used in the curriculum. Computers should be made available to teachers to enable them to practise and develop their growing skills.
3. A stimulus should be given to the development of educationally relevant software.

Government should encourage growing demand for hardware to be met through the commercial rather than public sector.

Stevenson had, in his report, outlined the three main elements in developing a seismic shift in the use of technology in school: infrastructure, content and practice. Without any one of these strategies, to make changes in teachers' approach was much less likely to succeed.

When the Labour Party came to power in 1997, they lost no time in implementing the recommendations of the Stevenson Report. The government's consultation paper *Connecting the Learning Society* (Department for Education and Employment 1997) was quickly published, setting out developments and ideas on implementing the development of a National Grid for Learning. The document also set some very demanding targets, which, if achieved, would revolutionize and modernize the use of technology in schools.

The Stevenson Report described the grid as a 'mosaic of interconnecting networks' that would provide a framework for connecting schools, training teachers and making good content widely available on line. It had three components: infrastructure, content and practice. The infrastructure included computers, printers, operating software and 'connectivity' (cabling, internal networks and Internet connections). Content on the grid included documents from a wide range of sources such as software developers and textbook publishers to resources produced by individual teachers and pupils. Practice represented what people did with the infrastructure and content, how they helped learning in the classroom and schools.

Special educational needs was seen very much as part of the National Grid for Learning developments. In designing the grid, the consultation report emphasized that 'The grid has the potential to make available additional support for special schools, pupils and pupils with special needs within mainstream schools and FE [further education], those being educated in hospital and teachers of learners with special needs' (Department for Education and Employment 1997: 15). As the National Grid has developed, there have been a number of initiatives directed at SEN.

Current developments

The British Educational and Communications Technology Agency (Becta) was set up by the New Labour Government in 1998 to replace the National Council for Educational Technology as the lead agency in supporting the government's programme to develop the National Grid for Learning (NGfL). It has a new and clear remit both to support other agencies and carry out its own work designed to ensure NGfL developments take account of the needs of pupils with SEN and their teachers. The

Agency supports and manages a number of initiatives, such as a range of mailing lists and electronic forums for teachers of pupils with SEN. These are very active discussion groups, bringing together practitioners to discuss issues and offer solutions to problems. At the time of writing, almost 2000 practitioners are members of over 40 SEN and inclusion lists at any one time.

With the Department for Education and Skills, Becta is developing a SEN centre including a comprehensive database of resources on the World Wide Web, which will enable those who want information to find it quickly and effectively. When complete, the site will enable any person working with pupils who have special needs to ask questions about teaching their pupils. As a result, they will receive a range of information on, for example, suggested resources, approaches to teaching, access to other sources of information and ways to contact colleagues who have similar issues. It will also enable those who supply this information to enter details of their resources, suggested approach or relevant practical information into the site. Providers and users will be brought together without the need to use longwinded and often imprecise free text searches through existing search engines. Inevitably as technology moves on, Becta will need to respond to new developments and use the ever increasingly clever technologies to ensure this and other developments serve teachers of pupils with SEN well.

From 2002 to 2004 Becta, on behalf of the SEN division of the Department for Education and Skills, is managing a project on communication aids. This initiative seeks to give support to pupils who have difficulty in understanding language, communicating verbally, developing reading skills and developing recording skills. The Communication Aids Project will help pupils who have communication difficulties by providing technology to help them access the curriculum, interact with others and support their transition to post-school provision. The project will be evaluated both for its impact on individuals and how technology raises standards of teaching and learning for the pupils it helps.

Up to 2004, New Opportunities Fund training for all serving teachers in the use of ICT in the curriculum includes a range of trainers offering SEN courses. Generally, reports on this specialist training has been well received and has increased the confidence and competence of teachers in using ICT with their pupils. Alongside this, the Teacher Training Agency has developed a needs-identification CD-ROM to support teachers of pupils with SEN in assessing their training needs. This software enables them to consider their own skills in using ICT with pupils with a range of learning needs. The CD-ROM shows ways in which ICT can help pupils access the curriculum, and how teachers can assess capabilities, support learning and demonstrate achievement.

The Department for Education and Skills, supported by Becta, have initiated schemes to provide SEN coordinators and LEA support services with laptops. Research into the use of speech recognition systems with pupils with SEN was completed by Becta in February 2000 and results and suggestions on good practice were disseminated. The development of managed services for schools, helping them to plan their ICT needs and purchase equipment over a number of years, including the purchase of equipment for use by pupils who may have SEN, has been a further development.

Broader developments in the use of technology are taking place as the twenty-first century rolls on. The vision of where we are going in schools is set out in the booklet *Transforming the Way We Learn* (Department for Education and Skills 2002). It advocates the harnessing of all current developments and driving them forward. As Estelle Morris, the former Secretary of State for Education, said:

> I firmly believe that, when used in the right circumstances, ICT has huge potential to engage pupils in ways that will help to realise their individual talents. It offers teachers new opportunities to develop their professional skills, whether in the classroom or in the virtual classroom.
>   (Department for Education and Skills 2002: 1)

This presages a daunting and demanding role for teachers and pupils and for the technologies they employ. Some of the initiatives that will make the vision a reality have been put in place. Others are new and just beginning to impact on practice or still under development and will be implemented in the coming years.

The government is committed to further investment in ICT over the coming years. From 2002 schools will be eligible for e-learning credits, additional funding that will enable them to procure high-quality educational content through a new Curriculum Online portal. However, if ICT is to remain an integral tool of high-standard teaching and learning, schools and LEAs themselves will need to take increasing responsibility for budgeting for ICT in a sustainable way.

The school of the future will be an ICT-rich environment including portable computers that can be deployed flexibly and linked to the school's networks through wireless technologies. They will have their own intranets with educational materials and information for pupils, teachers and parents from home over the Internet. Teachers will be confident in accessing a rich blend of educational content delivered through broadband connections to the Internet, digital television, satellite and DVD. Managed learning environment technologies will be available to provide personalized feedback and target setting.

Support mechanisms to help schools develop their approaches to technologies is becoming increasingly available through LEA regional consortia and centralized services. Examples of these include the new Independent Procurement Advisory Service. As schools gain more power over their ICT budgets, so they have to tangle with the increasingly complex issues of procurement, which is why the Service exists. It is intended to provide a framework that will help schools to choose between competing suppliers of ICT equipment and services. The organization itself will not make actual recommendations, but it will operate independently.

Conclusions

The picture at the beginning of the twenty-first century looks as healthy as at any time in the previous three decades. There is, however, no room for complacency. If history has taught us anything about ICT and SEN, then it should be that if we take our eyes off the ball we risk missing the goal. That goal for those of us working with pupils with SEN and particularly promoting the use of ICT with those learners is to ensure that new initiatives, whether ICT-based or not, include those to whom we are committed.

The National Grid for Learning is a marvellous opportunity and teachers need to be fully involved. The implementation of Curriculum 2000 and Curriculum Online offers new opportunities for access. We need to grasp and embrace those opportunities. Training needs to be designed to enhance the basic skills of using ICT in the curriculum for pupils with SEN that most teachers will have gained through training funded by the New Opportunities Fund. Resources developing as part of the National Grid for Learning must demonstrate good practice for those most vulnerable in an education system increasingly based on comparisons with the norm.

Since the 1970s, the use of technology in schools – particularly its use with pupils who have learning difficulties and disabilities – has been approached by successive governments with attitudes ranging from cautious to enthusiastic. Initiatives from the centre have, at various times, been designed to move things forward. However, these initiatives have often only partly provided the things schools require to make effective use of technology in meeting the needs of all pupils. Resources have been made available for computers in schools but developing the skills of teachers in using that equipment has been forgotten. Training has been made available, but once trained, teachers have found that inadequate access to equipment has meant that new-found skills could not be embedded in their everyday practice and often those skills were soon lost. However, I suggest that only when the three essential elements of provision – the right equipment, access to high-quality materials and ongoing practice-based training – are available together can we realistically expect teachers to integrate the use of ICT into their everyday teaching and learning.

Over the past 30 years, it has been the vigilance of those involved in ICT and SEN which has kept SEN always at the forefront of innovation, commitment and provision in harnessing technology for the benefit of all learners. Ian Taylor, a Minister at the Department for Trade and Industry in 1994, wrote in *TES Online* in February 2000 that the political environment for advancing the use of ICT in schools has improved enormously in recent years (Taylor 2000). He sees a revolution taking place and in that revolution those who recognize the potential for ICT in education will inevitably be the winners. Those committed to high-quality educational opportunity for pupils with SEN must continue to be vigilant to opportunity and creative in the application of technology to learning.

References

Coupland, J., Benzie, D., Butcher, P. *et al.* (1988) *The Rainbow Project*. Manchester: Microelectronics Education Support Unit ITMA Collaboration.

Department for Education and Employment (1997) *Connecting the Learning Society*. London: HMSO.

Department for Education and Skills (2002) *Transforming the Way We Learn: A Vision of the Future of ICT in Schools*. London: HMSO.

Department of Education and Science (1990) *A Report by HM Inspectorate: A Survey of the Microelectronics Education Support Unit (MESU) 1986–1989*. London: HMSO.

McKinsey and Co. (1997) *The Future of Information Technology in UK Schools*. London: McKinsey and Co.

Microelectronics Education Support Unit (1987) *Information Technology in Schools Seminar*. A day seminar to discuss the new DES strategy and the ESG (1988–90) proposals, 22 July. London: MESU.

Microelectronics Education Support Unit (1988) *Pipistrelle*. London: HMSO.

Stevenson, D. (1997) *The Stevenson Report: Information and Communications Technology in UK Schools – An Independent Inquiry*. London: Independent ICT in Schools Commission.

Tagg, B. (1995) *The Impact of Government Initiatives on IT Education in UK Schools*. Computer Education No. 81. Stafford: Computer Education Group.

Taylor, I. (2000) A tale of a PM and his mouse, *TES Online*, February. London: Times Educational Supplement.

3

FROM INTEGRATION TO INCLUSION: USING ICT TO SUPPORT LEARNERS WITH SPECIAL EDUCATIONAL NEEDS IN THE ORDINARY CLASSROOM

Lesley Rahamin

Introduction

Information and communications technology (ICT) has been used to support learners with special educational needs (SEN) in ordinary mainstream schools for many years. Known as assistive or enabling technology, it has adapted to developments in technology as well as to education policy changes for learners with different needs. In *Enabling Technology for Inclusion*, Blamires writes:

> Enabling Technology is about being helped to achieve something that could not have been achieved at all without that aid or without great personal effort. An individual may be enabled to learn something, say something, do something, create something, go somewhere or join in some activity.
>
> (Blamires 1999: 1)

In the 1970s, some learners who could not use a pencil effectively because of physical difficulties were using the keyboards of electric typewriters and early computers. Pupils found that hitting a key on a typewriter was easier than trying to form a letter with pencil and paper, and electric typewriters required less strength to produce letters than manual models. Computers had the access benefits of electric typewriters but they also had memory capacity. Software programs were written to improve text output by offering wordlists so that the writer could select a word or phrase from the list rather than type in every letter. Computers could also be adapted for input by switch. Pupils who did not have the physical strength or control to use a keyboard could make something happen on the screen by pressing a switch. Writing became possible by watching a highlight pass over an array of letters presented on screen. The writer pressed a switch when the highlight reached the required letter and predictive software helped the process by offering wordlists based on initial letters, grammar and frequency of previous use. Most pupils using this technology attended special schools where the size of the equipment and its lack of portability were not a problem. In ordinary schools, writers with special needs who were struggling would not often have the help of technology. The best most could expect would be someone to write for them.

In the 1980s, information technology (IT) equipment became smaller and more portable so that learners following the integration movement were able to use it in ordinary schools. Small electronic typewriters and word processors powered by batteries were developed so there was no longer any need for writers to sit next to the mains electricity supply. They could use their equipment in different teaching bases and work alongside their peers. But often pupils with special educational needs were the only ones using technology, and this sometimes created problems for those who did not want to be seen as different or who could not be provided with the technical support they required.

And now, at the beginning of the twenty-first century, modern computers are being brought into all schools to provide Internet access and software resources for all learners. Worldwide demands from disabled users have resulted in access features being incorporated into all hardware. All pupils and teachers are expected to be ICT literate and legislation is being passed to prevent disability discrimination and disadvantage in the workplace and in education.

In this chapter, I describe two scenarios, a decade apart, observed during my professional practice as a teacher specializing in the use of IT to support learners with special educational needs. The first is an example of a common situation that occurred as a result of the pro-integration movement of the 1980s, when isolated learners with SEN used individually assigned IT equipment in classrooms with very little other computer equipment or expertise. The second is an example from the present day and reflects changes in the technology, particularly the rapid development of electronic communication, as well as changes in attitude to the inclusion of learners with special needs in ordinary schools. They illustrate the progress from integration to inclusion.

In contrasting integration and inclusion, Rieser (1996) stated:

All forms of integration assume some form of assimilation of the disabled child into the mainstream school largely unchanged . . . Inclusion is not a static state like integration. It is a continuing process of school ethos change. It is about building a school community that accepts and values difference.

A model of integration

The 1981 Education Act introduced the term 'special educational need' for pupils who have a learning difficulty that requires special educational provision to be made (Department of Education and Science 1981). Statements of special educational needs are written to describe a pupil's needs and the provision that is to be made to meet those needs. The Act recommended that this provision should be made in ordinary schools wherever practicable and to facilitate that process local education authorities (LEAs) began to assign teachers and assistants to support individual learners, usually on a part-time basis. Most authorities employed non-teaching assistants who worked with the pupil at tasks set by the class or subject teacher. In 1986, I began working as an individual support teacher in a London primary school.

One child I supported was called Robert. I was his first individual support teacher and began working with him when he was 9 years old, continuing until he transferred to secondary school two years later. Robert had been born with cerebral palsy, resulting in muscle weakness throughout the left side of his body. Although his physical disabilities were not severe, a possible placement at a special school for learners with physical disabilities had been suggested to his parents, but Robert's older siblings had attended their local schools and his parents saw no reason why he should not do the same. As a result, a statement of special educational need was issued that continued his placement at the school with additional teaching support for two days a week.

Robert had progressed through the infant department with few problems. He was a confident child whose self-esteem had been built up by the loving support of his close-knit family. But later the situation began to change as he encountered increasing pressure to produce greater amounts of written work. Previously he had enjoyed handwriting but the effort involved in controlling his muscles proved tiring and the resulting script, although neat and legible, was much larger than that of his peers. This did not seem to concern him earlier but during his first year at junior school his enthusiasm waned and he became reluctant to write much more than a few lines, although he remained an active participant in oral class work. The school had some word-processing facilities and there was a system in place for sharing the few computers available, but Robert's teacher was unfamiliar with IT and rarely took up her class's allocation.

The LEA had a specialist support service to advise on using IT to support learners with special needs. It was based in a special school for learners with physical disabilities and its expertise had been in special schools, but with the move towards integration they had begun to extend their work to mainstream schools. Before I began working with Robert, the service had been asked to suggest alternatives to handwriting for him. They took into account the lack of IT capability available in school to support Robert and the absence of any individual learning support and loaned him a very simple electric typewriter. It was powered by mains electricity and extremely heavy and although it was not ideal, it was at least simple enough for him to use without support. However, Robert himself was reluctant to use the typewriter because he hated having to work next to the wall, isolated from his usual peer group. He also found typing very slow because he had never done any word processing before and was unfamiliar with the layout of the keyboard. In addition, Robert's Year 3 teacher did not encourage him to use the IT equipment because she said it made him look different. When he had difficulties she acted as a scribe for him or allowed him to submit work of a lower standard than that of which he was capable. Unfortunately, Robert's introduction to using assistive technology was as an isolated user in a classroom where very little use was made of technology. It proved to be a negative experience and before long the typewriter was assigned to a cupboard. Robert went back to handwriting a few words at his usual table until his teacher came and finished the writing for him.

I started working with Robert when he was 9 years old. He had a new class teacher who appreciated the children's differences and had high expectations of all of them. He used IT extensively across the curriculum, taking up not only his own allocation of shared computer access time but also moving into his classroom any computers that were not being used by other teachers. Word processing soon became an accepted augmentative writing tool for all children in the class. Robert benefited from shared access to the class word-processing equipment, but he also needed additional provision to give him more opportunities to write with a keyboard. After a review visit by an advisory teacher from the LEA support centre, Robert was loaned a lightweight, portable electronic typewriter. The machine was powered by rechargeable batteries so that he could now work anywhere he wanted. Having individual support meant that Robert had someone to help with maintenance, such as charging batteries and replacing printer ribbons. I was also able to give him short keyboard familiarity lessons during the first term to improve the speed of his text output. The result was that Robert developed a more positive attitude towards assistive technology and used a keyboard for almost all his writing needs. However, he was still an isolated user in a classroom where there was not enough IT equipment for it to be fully integrated across the curriculum. On occasions he would share the writing task with a friend, taking turns to use his typewriter, but occasionally he would reject the equipment and struggle with handwriting or dictate to a scribe.

After working with Robert and others, I became an advisory teacher for the LEA support centre, working across London to encourage the use of IT to support children with special educational needs. My observations of other situations at that time indicated that Robert was not alone in sometimes feeling that he did not want to use a writing tool that was different from his peers. Many learners with special educational needs found using ICT equipment in mainstream schools to be an isolating experience. For example, Michelle had a progressive condition that caused gradual weakening of her muscles. She attended a mainstream secondary school that she could access in her wheelchair. She was a very popular pupil and could have been helped by using a keyboard with a guard that she could rest her hands on. But she did not want to use anything that was different from her peers. As part of her statement of special needs she was assigned a special support assistant to help her around the school, but she steadfastly rejected any form of individual adult help. She had a close group of friends and with the agreement of the school they acted as scribes and helpers throughout the school day. The portable computer assigned to her stayed at home and was just used for homework. However, she was an enthusiastic learner in the ICT class and after gaining high grades at GCSE she took post-16 courses that involved technology. Michelle was quite happy to use the technology, but only if everyone else did.

Sometimes inappropriate equipment was assigned to children, perhaps provided by charities or well-meaning individuals who visited the children at home and made provision or recommendations without reference to the child's school. Teachers were then presented with expensive, complicated IT equipment and expected to learn how to incorporate it in their teaching without any training or support. Not surprisingly, the equipment found its way into a cupboard or was sent back home again. Other children were more fortunate and had a multi-professional assessment to decide on the most appropriate provision. Inputs from parents, teachers, therapists and support workers were added to the children's own voices, but such an array of professionals can be intimidating and perhaps some children were more inclined to agree with the suggestions of adults than express their true feelings.

Even when provided with equipment that suited the learner's home and school environments, problems occurred if there was a lack of on-going support to deal with technical and social problems. Training in the use and maintenance of the equipment was often given to support staff when it was allocated but this expertise was lost when staff changed. Unless new staff were trained, the learner was left without a key person to approach when difficulties occurred.

Changes in the educational infrastructure

Many of the changes in attitude and facilities have come about as a result of legislation. The 1981 Education Act has already been mentioned. It introduced the concept of special educational need and stated the principle that children should be educated in ordinary schools wherever practicable.

During the period covered by this chapter, the next important piece of legislation was the 1988 Education Reform Act (Department of Education and Science 1988). It gave statutory recognition to the rights of all pupils to a broad and balanced curriculum, including the National Curriculum, and emphasized the need for IT provision to overcome barriers of physical access. The National Curriculum Council's guidance booklet, *A Curriculum for All*, states:

> Some pupils with physical disabilities will need computers with adapted keyboards, word processors and other IT aids. Pupils with communication difficulties may need portable communication aids that use synthesised or recorded speech with overlays based on words, symbols or pictures.
>
> (National Curriculum Council 1989: 9)

The Act also made information technology a compulsory subject and the Orders embedded skills such as word processing and data retrieval in subjects across the curriculum. The decision on whether to use IT in the classroom was no longer that of individual teachers, because all learners were expected to be using it as a tool in their learning. Information technology was becoming a feature of all children's education across the curriculum, not just a means of access for those with disabilities.

In 1994, the *Code of Practice on the Identification and Assessment of Special Educational Needs* (Department for Education 1994) was published and included examples of how IT could be used as a learning tool for pupils with a wide range of special educational needs. The *Code* was revised in 2001 and re-emphasized the expectation that schools will take responsibility for using IT to address the needs of all pupils, before requesting specialized provision. For example, the requirement for primary schools is that:

> The SENCO and class teacher, together with curriculum, literacy and numeracy co-ordinators and external specialists, should consider a range of different teaching approaches and appropriate equipment and teaching materials, including the use of information technology.
>
> (Department for Education and Skills 2001: §5:58, p. 55)

A similar requirement is made for secondary schools.

In 1997, the UK returned a new government to power. The manifesto on which it had been elected placed great emphasis on the importance of increased funding for education. Soon after the change of government, the Department for Education and Employment published two consultation papers. In the first, *Connecting the Learning Society* (1997a), proposals were made for improving ICT literacy in schools in the light of the rapid expansion of electronic communication. In his introduction to the paper, the Prime Minister, Tony Blair, wrote: 'By 2002, all schools will be connected to the superhighway, free of charge; half a million teachers will be trained; and our children will be leaving school IT-literate, having been able to exploit the best that technology can offer' (Department for Education and Employment 1997a: 1).

The National Grid for Learning (NGfL) has been set up in response to the aim of the government to create 'a connected learning society in which learning is increasingly accessible and adapted to individual needs' (www.ngfl.gov.uk). A total of £657 million has been made available through the NGfL Standards Fund Grant to support new technology in schools for the four years 1998–2002, and a further £710 million for the two years 2002–2004 was announced in September 2000. Computer equipment for schools has been provided from central government funds and the NGfL website (www.ngfl.gov.uk) was launched in November 1998 as a gateway to educational resources on the Internet. Another element of the NGfL strategy focuses on the provision of ICT training for teachers and librarians. This has been done through the New Opportunities Fund programme to ensure that teachers and school librarians are equipped with the necessary knowledge, understanding and skills to use ICT effectively in teaching. The programme started in 1999 and ended in December 2003. The National Grid for Learning and New Opportunities Fund training programme should ensure that ICT is used effectively in schools to enhance the learning of all pupils.

Alongside a governmental commitment to increasing the use of ICT came a parallel proposal to increase the level and quality of the inclusion of learners with special educational needs in mainstream schools. The second 1997 consultation document, *Excellence for All Children: Meeting Special Educational Needs*, stated:

> By 2002 a growing number of mainstream schools will be willing and able to accept children with a range of SEN: as a consequence, an increasing proportion of those children with statements of SEN would currently be placed in special schools will be educated in mainstream schools.
>
> (Department for Education and Employment 1997b: 7)

The Disability Discrimination Act 1995 excluded measures to deal with discrimination in education; however, the Special Educational Needs and

Disability Act 2001 extended the legislation to schools. This amended Act states that schools have a duty not to treat disabled pupils less favourably than their peers. In addition, they have a duty to make reasonable adjustments to avoid putting disabled pupils at a substantial disadvantage. This example of what might be considered a reasonable adjustment is given in the 2002 *Code of Practice for Schools*:

> Example 6.14A
> A large secondary school is opening a special unit for pupils with speech and language impairments. They plan to include the pupils from the unit in mainstream lessons. One of the challenges is how to enable the children in the unit to follow the timetable. They might otherwise be at a substantial disadvantage. The school has an established 'buddy system' as part of its anti-bullying policy. After discussions with pupils, parents and the speech and language specialist teacher, the school extends its buddy system. It provides training for additional volunteer buddies to guide the disabled pupils from class to class. This is likely to be a reasonable adjustment that they should take.
> (Disability Rights Commission 2002: 59)

Another example from the same publication highlights a situation that might be unlawful:

> Example 4.21B
> A secondary school hosts a special unit for pupils with a visual impairment. The school is already appropriately equipped for enlarging text and providing Braille versions of documents for pupils who use Braille. When the pupils are working in the unit, all information is provided in a range of formats at the beginning of the lesson. When they are working in mainstream classes in the school, the school regularly fails to provide information in time to be transferred into different formats before the lesson. Not providing the information in time leaves the disabled children unable to refer to written information during the lesson, whilst their non-disabled peers can. This is likely to constitute a substantial disadvantage in comparison with non-disabled pupils. The failure to take reasonable steps to prevent this disadvantage is likely to be unlawful.
> (Disability Rights Commission 2002: 56)

Although IT is not specifically mentioned in either of these examples, using software to produce symbols that can be displayed alongside text would be a time-saving way to make the information available to all pupils, including those for whom unsupported text is not accessible. The second example shows how teaching and support staff have a duty to make sure that the provisions provided for the pupil are made available to them when they need them.

A model of inclusion

When I began my work with Robert, it was as a support teacher assigned to him for a one-to-one relationship, teaching two days every week. My role was to ensure that he understood what was required and that he completed the work assigned. It soon became apparent that this was neither necessary nor beneficial. We found that such a model was counter-productive because it encouraged the learner to be dependent on an adult, rather than develop strategies for progression when that support was withdrawn. Much more productive was a method of cooperative working with the class teacher, differentiating tasks for individuals but working with the whole class to ensure that everyone who needed help was getting it. I learned to step back and let Robert move on.

I took a step further away from working in the classroom when I accepted a post as an advisory teacher in ICT and SEN with an LEA specialist support service. My job was to assess the ICT needs of learners referred to the service and provide them with appropriate equipment. I would then deliver training to the learner, parents and teachers in its use and suggest how it could be used to provide improved access to the curriculum. Some of the children I supported attended a school with a high proportion of learners with individual needs. It was built in the mid-1990s as part of a new development in an urban brown-field area. The remnants of old industry had been demolished and the site rebuilt with a mixture of houses and flats. Some were rented, either from the local council or from private landlords, and some were owner-occupied. The area is considered a desirable place to live with good transport links and leisure, industrial and shopping facilities.

The school buildings were designed to be completely accessible by learners in wheelchairs and those with hearing and visual difficulties. The staff of the school have a commitment to the inclusion of learners with special needs and welcome children with a range of learning difficulties and physical and sensory disabilities. Most of the pupils come from the immediate local area but because the school was designed to be fully accessible to disabled pupils, it is also popular with parents who want their children to attend mainstream school but whose own local schools are not accessible. Visiting specialist teachers and health staff support individual children and deliver training to teachers in the school.

The LEA that maintains the school has had a commitment to improving the IT provision in its schools for many years and, combined with recent national funding initiatives, this has resulted in a high level of computer provision as well as Internet access. Staff have undergone training in ICT literacy and are now incorporating it across the curriculum. Their positive attitude to inclusion has ensured that the access needs of all children are met by fitting the computers with a range of utilities:

- All computers are positioned on adjustable trolleys so that the height can be altered for children in wheelchairs.
- Keyguards are available to fit over regular keyboards to stop unwanted key presses by children whose hand movements are unsteady.
- Trackballs are available for children whose hand-control difficulties make standard mice difficult to use.
- Touch screens are fitted over some monitors to give a more direct method of input for children with multiple learning difficulties. Navigation and selection are done by moving a finger across the membrane of the touch screen.
- A keyboard delay is set to give the children longer to remove their fingers from the keys before the characters start repeating.
- Screen cursors are enlarged so that all children can locate them more easily, not just those with visual difficulties.
- One computer uses a high-contrast display so that a child with visual difficulties can see it better.
- One computer has the Sticky Key facility switched on so that a child with limited strength in one hand can operate the keyboard without having to hold down two keys at the same time.
- All computers have 'talking' word processors installed so that children with low vision or literacy difficulties can use their text-to-speech facilities to support their reading. The default font used is a bold Arial font in size 18 settings, but the children all know how to change it if they find that uncomfortable.
- Some computers have symbol processors installed. They add symbols automatically to words as they are typed, enabling staff to produce materials that are more accessible to learners who need support to read text.
- Overlay keyboards are used extensively throughout the school. One child uses an overlay with the QWERTY keyboard printed on it in high-contrast letters that she can see more easily. Other children use overlays with word banks to support their writing, pressing areas of the keyboard to enter whole words or phrases to supplement their regular typing.

By ensuring that all its pupils have access to enabling technologies, the school is providing a more inclusive environment than was available previously. But although these utilities are available to them, I noticed that the learners with special educational needs did not always choose to use them. Sometimes they preferred to work cooperatively with their peers, sharing individual strengths and supporting one another in overcoming difficulties. An inclusive educational environment empowers them by giving them the choice.

Robert was not empowered by the class teacher who wrote for him rather than valuing what he could do. He soon got the message that his work was not good enough. He was empowered by the teacher who expected appropriate standards for him and by having the IT tools provided that would assist him. If he were at school today, he would not be an isolated user of IT. Word processing, computer art and data processing are skills that all learners are encouraged to use and would not present barriers to his physical limitations.

But access to the technology is not all that is required. The way in which information is presented must be appropriate to the learner. A learner can read along with a talking book, but if the content is not relevant or interesting, there will not be engagement. A pupil can copy and paste text from a web page into a symbol word processor, but if the comprehension level is not appropriate, learning will not take place.

In *Enabling Technology for Inclusion*, Blamires (1999: 6) writes that enabling technology is not just about access, it's about engagement and inclusion. With appropriate enabling utilities, resources designed on universal access principles and the conviction that children with special needs have a right to a broad and balanced curriculum, we can ensure that they have access, engagement and inclusion.

References

Blamires, M. (ed.) (1999) *Enabling Technology for Inclusion*. London: Paul Chapman.

British Educational Communications and Technology Agency (2001) *Information sheet: National Grid for Learning* (http://www.becta.org.uk/technology/infosheets/html/ngfl.html).

Department for Education (1994) *Code of Practice on the Identification and Assessment of Special Educational Needs*. London: HMSO.

Department for Education and Employment (1997a) *Connecting the Learning Society: National Grid for Learning (NGfL)*. London: HMSO.

Department for Education and Employment (1997b) *Excellence for All Children: Meeting Special Educational Needs* (Summary). London: HMSO.

Department for Education and Skills (2001) *Special Educational Needs Code of Practice*. London: DfES.

Department of Education and Science (1981) *Education Act*. London: HMSO.

Department of Education and Science (1988) *Education Reform Act*. London: HMSO.

Disability Rights Commission (2001) *The Special Educational Needs and Disability Act*. London: Disability Rights Commission.

Disability Rights Commission (2002) *Code of Practice for Schools: Disability Discrimination Act 1995, Part 4*. London: TSO.

National Curriculum Council (1989) *A Curriculum for All*. York: National Curriculum Council.

Rieser, R. (1996) Unpublished notes from a talk given by *Disability in Education*. London: SENJIT, University of London Institute of Education.

4

USING COMPUTER-BASED ASSESSMENT TO IDENTIFY LEARNING PROBLEMS

Chris Singleton

Assessment is an integral and essential part of all good teaching. Unless teachers are aware of their students' progress, decisions about appropriate strategies for developing learning cannot be made. 'Summative assessment' constitutes a formal record of the curriculum-related achievements of students at the culmination of a stage or programme of study. 'Formative assessment' is an on-going activity during the learning process by which teachers can evaluate individual students' progress and provide appropriate feedback that will help to optimize learning and understanding. Formative assessment is a much more fluid process that is mostly carried out informally, with the teacher noting that students who have failed to reach expected levels of attainment will require additional learning to bring them up to scratch. Such evaluations, which are largely based on criteria laid down in the curriculum, may be derived from observation of the students' work, from results of class tests and interim examinations, or perhaps from outcomes of statutory assessments such as Standardized Achievement Tests (SATs). These sources of information may tell the teacher about the extent of a student's deficiencies and, possibly, in which aspects of a given subject these deficiencies lie. Rarely will such information give clues about the *causes* of a student's difficulties. While teachers get to know much about their students from their close and frequent contact with them, it would aid them considerably if there were effective techniques of diagnostic assessment that teachers could use on a regular basis.

The *Special Educational Needs Code of Practice* (Department for Education and Skills 2001) places a duty on *all* educators, whether in mainstream or special schools, or in early education settings, to play a part in the identification and provision for pupils with special educational needs (SEN). Particular responsibilities are carried by special educational needs coordinators (SENCOs). The *Code of Practice* stresses the vital importance of early identification of SEN: 'The earlier action is taken, the more responsive the child is likely to be, and the more readily can intervention be made without undue disruption to the organisation of the school' (§5.11, p. 46 and §6:10, p. 60). To help identify pupils with SEN, schools are encouraged to employ a variety of strategies, including the use of screening or assessment tools (see §5:13 and §6:12), but it is stressed that 'Assessment should not be regarded as a single event but rather as a continuous process' (§5.11, p. 46 and §6:10, p. 60). Early identification of problems encountered in learning – before these develop into outright failure – could enable the teacher to intervene within the mainstream classroom, rather than having to resort to withdrawal for specialist intervention. The former is educationally desirable, as the *Code of Practice* emphasizes, but it is also more cost-effective as well as being more ethical, since it does not rely on waiting for children to fail and thus tries to avoid the emotional and motivational repercussions of failure. However, *all* successful intervention – but especially *early* intervention – depends on good diagnostic information. It is not enough to know simply that a pupil has problems in learning. To shape intervention effectively, it is necessary to *understand* the problems and their ramifications on the pupil's learning behaviour. Such understanding should then be used to develop a more specifically targeted intervention.

Ideally, therefore, to teach well, all educators should not only be monitoring their pupils' progress and attainment and identifying any problems encountered in learning, but they should also be investigating those problems diagnostically. Unfortunately, diagnostic assessment is time-consuming and not easy. Applying informal methods of diagnostic assessment usually depends on many years of experience, especially in teaching pupils with SEN. Formal diagnostic assessment typically involves mastery of several complex assessment tools: skills in which educational psychologists are trained, but few teachers get this opportunity. Fortunately, in recent years the development of computer-based diagnostic assessment tools has come to the aid of teachers, which have enabled both the easier identification and deeper understanding of children's learning problems as well as the development of educational solutions that can be effective in the mainstream classroom. In this chapter, I discuss these tools and their potential for teachers.

The advantages of computer-based assessment

Computer-based assessment (CBA) has been defined as 'any psychological assessment that involves the use of digital technology to collect, process and report the results of that assessment' (British Psychological Society 1999: 1). CBA is employed extensively in business and industry, especially for the purposes of recruitment, selection and promotion. In education, it is used widely for selection at college level (particularly in the USA, but also in several other countries), for monitoring progress in many areas of the curriculum and for 'paper-less' examinations. In the UK, one of the most notable applications of CBA is within integrated learning systems (ILS), which are computer-based training programs designed to provide learning practice for large numbers of pupils simultaneously via networked computer systems. The computer has to assess the progress of each pupil to map a route for them through the learning materials offered by the program (for a review, see Wood *et al.* 1999; see also Chapter 5). It is not the purpose of this chapter to review the use of CBA in education: this has been done elsewhere (see Singleton 1997b, 2001). However, it is worth examining the benefits that CBA can bring to special needs education, particularly in relation to diagnostic assessment of learning problems.

Savings in time, labour and cost

With CBA, the computer does most of the work of assessment, including administering items, recording responses and scoring results. Hence labour and cost savings when using CBA compared with conventional assessments delivered by human personnel can be significant. In comparisons of conventional and computerized versions of tests, teachers generally prefer the latter, mainly because results are immediately available, which saves time in scoring responses and calculating standard scores (Woodward and Rieth 1997). Time savings are considerable when CBA is *adaptive* – that is, where the difficulty of items selected from a test bank is varied in response to the pupil's progress on the test. The term 'adaptive testing' refers to any technique that modifies the nature of the test in response to the performance of the test taker. This can be achieved in a variety of ways, although typically it is used in connection with tests that are developed by means of Item Response Theory (Hambleton and Swaminathan 1985). Conventional tests are *static* instruments, fixed in their item content, item order and duration. By contrast, CBA can be *dynamic*. Since the computer can score performance at the same time as item presentation, it can modify the test accordingly, tailoring it more precisely to the capabilities of the pupil taking the test. In conventional tests, for some part of the time, the pupil's abilities are not being assessed with any great precision because the items are either too difficult or too easy (which can easily lead to frustration and/or boredom). In a computerized adaptive test, however, because the program contains information about the difficulty of every item in the item bank (based on pass rates in the standardization population), the individual taking the test can be moved swiftly to that zone of the test that will most efficiently discriminate his or her capabilities. This makes the whole process speedier, more reliable, more efficient and often more acceptable to the person being tested. It has been shown that an adaptive CBA can take only a quarter of the time to administer than an equivalent conventional test (Olsen 1990).

Adaptive testing has been implemented in the Lucid Assessment System for Schools (LASS), a multi-functional assessment suite used for both diagnosing and monitoring pupils' progress. There are two versions: LASS Junior (Thomas *et al.* 2001) for ages 8:0–11:11 and LASS Secondary (Horne *et al.* 1999) for ages 11:0–15:11. Both of these programs include adaptive tests of reading, spelling, memory, phonological processing and nonverbal reasoning. In these tests, adaptivity is usually achieved by means of the 'probe technique', in which the pupil is first given a series of items of sharply increasing difficulty ('probes'). As soon as the pupil fails a probe item, the main part of the test commences at a level determined by the difficulty of the last correct probe item. The program can then move the pupil back to easier items or forward to more difficult items if it turns out that the probe resulted in the test being started at an inappropriate level (for example, due to passing or failing probe item by chance). Finally, when a set criterion is reached (for example, failing a given number of items consecutively), the test is automatically discontinued.

An alternative approach to adaptive testing was employed in CoPS Baseline Assessment, an on-entry assessment program for children aged 4:0–5:6 (Singleton *et al.* 1998). The challenges in developing this program were considerable, since to be accredited by the Qualifications and Curriculum Authority for use in schools in England, strict criteria had to be adhered to. These criteria specified assessment in four key components of the early learning curriculum (communication skills, literacy, mathematics, and personal and social development) and a total assessment time of no longer than 20 minutes. This meant that assessment of each component could not take more than 5 minutes. It was found that young children could not complete more than about 16 computer-based test items in 5 minutes, and so an adaptive algorithm was developed to overcome the problem. Banks of 56 items of known difficulty were created for both the literacy and mathematics modules, each being subdivided into eight different skill/concept areas (for example, for the literacy module these included knowledge about print, letter recognition, phonological awareness, and simple reading and spelling), with seven items of increasing difficulty in each area. The child attempts only two items from each area, and progress through the test is determined by item-to-item performance, so that the computer administers items that are most appropriate for that child's ability level. The success of this approach was demonstrated by the finding that the adaptive form of the test (16 items) correlated highly (0.81) with the full form (56 items). Baseline scores derived from the adaptive form were also found to give good prediction of development in both literacy and mathematics over the first year of schooling (correlations ≈ 0.75) (Singleton *et al.* 1999). Although government regulations regarding baseline assessment in state schools in England were changed in 2002, removing the requirement for on-entry assessment, CoPS Baseline Assessment is still widely used elsewhere, including independent schools across the UK, state schools in Scotland, and British and International schools around the world. This illustrates the advantages of adaptive test theory in the creation of new assessment tools that are brief enough to be practicable for teachers and stimulating to young children, while still yielding results that satisfy educational needs and meet psychometric standards. CoPS Baseline provides a snapshot of the child's level of development in the component areas at the time of school entry. Although not primarily intended for diagnostic purposes, it can nevertheless identify children who are weak in various aspects of learning and thus can be used in decision making about subsequent teaching and learning approaches for such children. Hence it can have certain limited diagnostic value. However, the similarly named program Lucid Cognitive Profiling System (CoPS), with which CoPS Baseline Assessment should not be confused, is designed specifically for diagnostic purposes. The specific features of this CBA are discussed later in this chapter.

Lucid Adult Development Screening (LADS) is a computerized test designed to screen for dyslexia from age 16 and older in further and higher education and in many other settings (Singleton *et al.* 2002). In this test, adaptivity is achieved by means of the CAST technique (Computerized Adaptive Sequential Testing), in which blocks of items of similar difficulty are administered sequentially (Drasgow and Olson-Buchanan 1999). LADS incorporates assessment of speeded lexical access, phonological coding and working memory, skills that are typically weak in dyslexia (Snowling 2000; Singleton 2002), even in bright adults who have developed excellent compensatory techniques and who have been educated to a high level (see Singleton 1999. ('Speeded tests' are ones in which a set time is allowed for the assessment.) In LADS, the pupil's performance on each block determines which block will be administered next, until the program has established the pupil's maximum level of functioning for that test. The timing of item presentation is also variable, which enables the test to take account of speed-of-processing deficits that have been observed in dyslexia (Wolf and O'Brien 2001). The result is a relatively short test (20 minutes) that is easy to administer and non-threatening to test-takers, but which still achieves a high level of accuracy.

Increased test motivation

Pupils with SEN have been found to display negative responses to conventional tests given in pen-and-paper format or administered by a human assessor (Wade and Moore 1993). By contrast, many studies have reported that children and adults, particularly those with low ability or who have 'failed' educationally, feel less threatened by CBA than by conventional assessment and hence prefer the former (Watkins and Kush 1988; Singleton 1997b). In an adaptive test, pupils are not exposed to items that would be ridiculously easy or impossibly difficult for them, which also enhances test motivation. In a study comparing CBA of verbal and non-verbal ability with assessment of the same cognitive domains using conventional methods, Singleton (2001) found that children displayed a clear preference for the CBA over the conventional assessment. In part, this was because the CBA was designed to be attractive and enjoyable (including use of colourful graphics, animation and sound) and, consequently, was widely perceived by the children to be 'more fun'. Similar preferences were expressed by teenagers (both male and female) being assessed on LASS Secondary, where 72 per cent of those assessed preferred the computer tests to equivalent conventional tests.

It is important to appreciate that although able and successful pupils may be self-motivated during a conventional assessment, many pupils with SEN are not. Assessment is likely to be perceived as yet another potential failure experience for them and therefore their motivation and interest are low. A human assessor must provide the motivation. In CBA, there is no human assessor to encourage the child and therefore motivation is dependent on the content and structure of the program. CBA that is perceived by pupils to be boring, unstimulating and uninteresting will not elicit strong test motivation and, consequently, the validity of the results will be questionable. Delivery of CBA as games, or the use of amusing animated sequences as rewards for test completion, may be viewed by some teachers with suspicion. These devices, both pioneered in the diagnostic assessment program CoPS Cognitive Profiling System (Singleton *et al.* 1996), may be thought of as a gimmick or 'edu-tainment' when in reality they are essential to keep children motivated and on task in the absence of a human assessor.

For older individuals who feel that they have 'failed' at school, confidence during an assessment tends be very fragile. Being assessed by a teacher (or another adult who takes on a role equivalent to that of a teacher, such as a psychologist) can evoke painful memories of humiliation at school, which can result in complete loss of motivation or emotional breakdown. A CBA (such as LADS) is usually perceived as less threatening than conventional assessment, and enables adults to be assessed in a confidential and non-stressful manner (Singleton and Horne, in press). Similar findings have been reported by Horne *et al.* (2002b), where teenagers preferred the computer tests in LASS Secondary to equivalent conventional tests, and this preference was much more pronounced in pupils with SEN. Of the non-SEN pupils, 67 per cent preferred CBA, but of the pupils with SEN, 92 per cent preferred CBA.

Greater precision and standardization of administration

In conventional assessment, some variation in test administration is inevitable. In CBA, by contrast, the test is *exactly the same* for all recipients, which helps to improve reliability of measurement. With CBA, the timing and delivery of test items and measurement of responses is much more precise than in conventional assessment. This is particularly important where timing is critical, for example in the presentation of items in memory tests or in speeded tests.

Is CBA as good as conventional assessment?

Despite the considerable advantages outlined in the previous section, some teachers may feel that CBA is somehow a 'second best' – something to be used because it is quick and easy, and because children find it enjoyable – rather than a technique to be valued in its own right. Sceptics may argue that human assessors will always be better than computers because they can detect aspects of performance that the computer cannot possibly be aware of, such as the state of health of the pupil, their level of confidence or attention, or the effort that they are putting in. Some important aspects of behaviour generally determined by observation, such as social and emotional behaviour, cannot be directly assessed by computerized means. Abilities that depend on reading and understanding large amounts of text are also problematic for CBA because of the difficulties that some people experience when reading text on a computer screen, which results in reading from the screen being 20–30 per cent slower than reading from paper (Dillon 1992) and for some individuals can lead to symptoms of visual discomfort (Wilkins 1986). Tasks that require use of expressive language (including speech production and phonological skills) are also problematic for CBA. However, imaginative CBA design can circumvent many of these problems. Assessment of social and emotional behaviour is amenable to CBA using on-screen questionnaires and rating scales (an example of this is found in the program CoPS Baseline Assessment). When large amounts of text have to be read, these can be provided in conventional printed format with the questions being delivered by the computer and responses being made via the keyboard (or mouse or other suitable input device). Singleton *et al.* (1995) developed a computerized reading comprehension test for primary age children where the text was presented in conventional illustrated book form, while the child listened to comprehension questions spoken by the computer and made responses using the mouse. Although the accuracy and sophistication of voice recognition systems has developed substantially in recent years, we still await the introduction of voice recognition software that is sufficiently reliable for all pupils to be assessed by speaking to the computer. Nevertheless, some aspects of language that are conventionally assessed by verbal interaction are still susceptible to CBA. Two examples are the phonological awareness and phonemic discrimination tests in CoPS Cognitive Profiling System (Singleton *et al.* 1996), in which the language skills are assessed by the children using the mouse to click on objects corresponding to spoken words that have rhyming or alliterative features, or on characters who have spoken the sounds correctly. The tests in CoPS show significant concurrent and prospective correlations with equivalent conventional tests, and the whole suite was also validated by means of statistical analysis of prospective longitudinal data predicting literacy difficulties and dyslexia from ages 5 to 8 years (Singleton *et al.* 2000).

It should be self-evident that no psychometric test can supply all the information that a teacher requires to make sensible educational decisions. The test results must be integrated with other information about the pupil, including how he or she behaves in class, the effort put into classwork and homework, and any emotional problems being experienced. But these provisos apply to all psychometric tests, not just to computer-based assessments. The particular advantage of psychometric tests is that they can provide objective information about the pupil's performance compared with population norms, and so remove some of the limitations that might otherwise cloud educational judgements. As noted above, computerized tests not only make assessment easier for the teacher and often more acceptable to the pupil, they also enable many aspects of assessment to be more sophisticated and thus more useful in diagnostic contexts.

One way of determining whether CBA is as good as conventional assessment is to make a direct comparison of the two using the same sample. Singleton (2001) reported a study in which children were given conventional and computerized tests of verbal and non-verbal ability. Ninety children aged 6–7 years were administered CBA of verbal ability (verbal concepts) and non-verbal ability (mental rotation), and the scores were compared with measures of verbal and non-verbal ability derived from conventional psychological assessment. The results revealed an expected pattern of significant intercorrelations, indicating that the different assessment formats did not significantly affect the ability being assessed. Similar findings have been reported by Horne *et al.* (2002a). Contrary to some suggestions that computer activities may favour boys (see Crook 1994; Singleton *et al.* 1999), no gender differences were found in either the conventional or computer assessment formats. Horne *et al.* (2002c) reported a study of 176 secondary school pupils (102 boys and 74 girls). No significant gender differences were found in any of the tests in the CBA suite LASS Secondary.

In many respects, CBA can offer *better* assessment than conventional approaches. In addition to being able to make use of game formats to deliver assessments, thereby being able to assess children who would otherwise be difficult to assess effectively by conventional means, CBA enables assessment of many aspects of performance that would be impractical to measure conventionally. An example is response time, which is tricky for human assessors to control or measure but which can easily be managed by CBA. An example of a CBA in which response time is central to the assessment is the Dyscalculia Screener (Butterworth 2001). Dyscalculia is a specific learning difficulty in mathematics, in which children experience great difficulty understanding simple number concepts, lack an intuitive grasp of numbers and have problems learning number facts and procedures. Even when these children produce a correct answer or use a correct method, they tend to do so mechanically and without confidence (Butterworth 1999). With the Dyscalculia Screener, diagnosis of dyscalculia is achieved by measuring response times to test items involving enumerating, understanding number size, numerals and simple arithmetic, in comparison with basic reaction time. Particular profiles on this test correspond to dyscalculia, but since the program gives information on performance in various sub-tests, in some cases the information could, in principle, be used to help plan intervention.

Use of response time in CBA enables a clear diagnostic distinction to be made between children whose performance is accurate and fast, those who are accurate but much slower in their responses, and those who are fast but inaccurate (the latter may be because of attentional problems or high impulsivity). One diagnostic program that incorporates this feature is CoPS Cognitive Profiling System (Singleton *et al.* 1996). Such data enable the teacher to gain an understanding of the child's speed of information processing in different modalities. When delivered by conventional means, speeded tests typically specify an overall time for a test comprising many items. It will not be possible to deduce from the results of such tests which items were hard and thus took the child longer and which were easier and hence took a shorter time. All that will be known is the overall number of items that the pupil passed in the time allowed, and which items were passed, failed or unattempted. However, in a speeded CBA, it is possible to control the time allowed separately for each individual item, thus providing more sophisticated diagnostic information about the child's abilities (or inabilities).

Another example of assessment that is impractical by conventional means is that of allowing more than one answer. In a multiple-choice test, if a child gets the answer wrong it may be helpful to know whether allowing them a second choice would enable them to get the answer right. A child who gets the right answer on the second choice knows more than one who gets neither the first or the second choice right. With CBA, the computer can score the first choice before deciding whether to offer a second choice; that option is not practical in conventional assessment (for a report on a study of this approach, see Singleton *et al.* 1995). Furthermore, because responses can be by means other than speech or writing, CBA can provide for the assessment of pupils with severe physical disabilities or profound sensory impairments (for a review, see Woodward and Rieth 1997).

Identification of learning problems using CBA

In educational contexts, diagnostic assessment refers to any process that seeks to identify componential factors in an individual's cognitive abilities or educational attainments in order to understand why that individual experiences difficulties in learning. The purpose of this identification is to enable the teacher to select or develop the most appropriate techniques for addressing that individual's difficulties and for promoting more effective learning. Sometimes these techniques will involve *training* (for example, in decoding strategies for children with poor phonic skills); sometimes *practice* is the main requirement (for example, in reading text to develop fluency in word recognition and increase comprehension); and sometimes *support* is the principal objective (for example, word processing with speech feedback for a child with poor writing skills). Often, a combination of these approaches is needed. To decide which approach or strategy is most likely to be beneficial, it is necessary to have fairly detailed information about the nature of the problem. For example, if the teacher assumes that the pupil needs more practice at reading text without first checking that he or she can use phonic strategies to decode unfamiliar words, then such practice may result in frustration for the child and not lead to improved reading comprehension. Furthermore, if the teacher establishes that a child cannot decode unfamiliar words, it will also be important to try to discover why the child has poor phonic skills. If the fundamental cause is cognitive, such as poor phonological processing ability and/or poor working memory (both of which can be determined by diagnostic assessment), this will have different implications for subsequent improvement than if the problem is due mainly to the way in which phonics has been taught in the first place (for example, too fast and with little monitoring of individual progress).

In diagnostic assessment, it is helpful to distinguish two broad types of component factor: *generic factors*, which contribute to a variety of general problems in learning (for example, language skills, memory and perception), and *specific factors*, which impinge directly on certain delineated aspects of learning (for example, phonic and word recognition skills on learning to read, or place value and number fact knowledge on learning arithmetic). Secondary learning problems may be consequential upon difficulties in specific skills (for example, poor phonic skills affect the development of reading, which, in turn, has repercussions on the ability to cope with new vocabulary in various parts of the curriculum).

A longitudinal CBA study reported by Singleton *et al.* (2000) showed that cognitive assessment by means of computer-delivered tests is a valid and practical method for identifying children who are at risk of reading difficulties. The tests in the computer suite CoPS Cognitive Profiling System (Singleton *et al.* 1996) were administered at age 5 and were later found to correlate significantly with conventional reading measures given at age 6 and 8 years. CoPS is a suite of eight computer-based assessments that measure various cognitive abilities, including visual and auditory memory, phonological awareness and phoneme discrimination. The CoPS tests of auditory memory and phonological awareness yielded the highest correlation coefficients with reading development, but phoneme discrimination was found to be a significant predictor of phonic skills and listening skills. The CoPS measures of visual memory were also significantly correlated with later word and text reading. Regression analyses revealed that the CoPS tests given at age 5 accounted for 31 per cent of the variance in reading scores at age 6 and 37 per cent of the variance in reading scores at age 8. Conventional assessments of general ability perform less well than the cognitive measures as early predictors of reading attainment, and CoPS was found to outperform the conventional tests on all counts in predicting poor readers at age 8. The numbers of false-positives and false-negatives were low or zero for the CoPS measures, while the conventional tests produced an unacceptably high number of false-positives and a moderate number of false-negatives. ['False-positives' were those children predicted to have problems in literacy who subsequently did not have problems, while 'false-negatives' were those who were *not* predicted to have problems who subsequently did have problems in literacy. For further discussion of issues in accuracy in educational screening, see Singleton (1997a).] It was concluded that as components of a diagnostic procedure for identifying children at risk of reading failure, the conventional tests employed in this study would be unsatisfactory and inferior to cognitive measures such as those in CoPS.

Horne *et al.* (2002b) reported a study in which 176 pupils aged 11–15 attending 12 different schools were tested by their teachers using LASS Secondary. In total, 129 pupils had no identified special educational needs, 30 had diagnosed dyslexia and 17 were on the SEN register for reasons other than dyslexia. Significant differences were found between the dyslexic and the non-SEN group on CBA measures of reading, spelling, auditory sequential memory, phonic skills (nonword reading) and phonological processing (syllable segmentation). This follows the expected cognitive pattern for dyslexia reported in the literature (see Snowling 2000;

Singleton 2002). The 'other SEN' group also scored lower than the non-SEN group on all of the above five tests as well as on CBA measures of reasoning and visual memory. By contrast, there were no significant differences between the dyslexic and the non-SEN group on CBA measures of reasoning or visual memory. Hence pupils' profiles on LASS Secondary enabled a clear differentiation between pupils in the three groups, demonstrating the utility of CBA in diagnostic assessment in the classroom. In fact, in accurately identifying the dyslexic pupils, LASS Secondary outperformed conventional assessments also used in the study.

Case studies

The investigations reported above demonstrate the validity of CBA in diagnostic assessment. However, statistical findings frequently fail to put across the practical benefits of this approach for teachers. The following case studies illustrate how CBA can help the teacher to identify both generic and specific factors that are hindering learning, and to develop appropriate strategies for learning and teaching to address these.

Ewan, aged 6 years 7 months

After a little over 18 months in school, Ewan was making very slow progress in literacy. He could not reliably recognize all the letters of the alphabet and could write fewer than a third of them. His formation of letters that he was able to write was generally very poor. He could read a few simple words (including his name). He could write his name but his attempts at writing other words were mostly indecipherable. Yet he was orally bright, responded eagerly to the teacher's questions and played a lively part in class discussion. About 6 months ago his teachers had begun to suspect that Ewan was dyslexic, but he had not yet been seen by an educational psychologist. Given the assumption of dyslexia, it was regarded as problematic to attempt phonic work with him before a more solid base of letter- and word-recognition skills had been established, and so teaching focused mainly on Ewan's visual skills, in the attempt to build up a basic sight vocabulary. This approach had not worked. Ewan was then tested using the CoPS Cognitive Profiling System (Singleton *et al.* 1996), described earlier in this chapter. This is a CBA that assesses cognitive abilities that are critical to development of literacy, such as phonological awareness, phoneme discrimination, and auditory and visual memory (Singleton 2002). Ewan found the CoPS tests fun and was enthusiastic about them. His results are shown in Figure 4.1.

The tests in CoPS are generally known by their shorthand names, but it is not necessary to go into full details here. Broadly, the first four tests (shown on the left-hand side of Figure 4.1) assess various aspects of

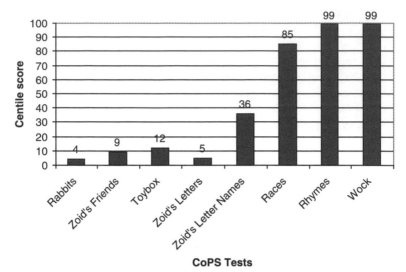

Figure 4.1   CoPS cognitive profiling system results for Ewan,
aged 6 years 7 months.

visual memory, while the remaining four tests (shown on the right-hand side of Figure 4.1) measure auditory/verbal abilities, including phonological awareness ('Rhymes'), phoneme discrimination ('Wock'), auditory sequential memory ('Races') and auditory-visual associative memory ('Zoid's Letter Names').

Ewan's CoPS results came as a surprise to his teachers. As well as showing a clear problem with remembering visual information (which had not been suspected before the assessment), they also confounded the assumption of dyslexia. Typically, children with dyslexia have difficulties mainly in phonological processing and auditory working memory (Snowling 2000; Singleton 2002), but Ewan's skills in these areas were extremely good. Arguably, Ewan falls within a category that might be termed 'visual dyslexia', although that rather vague nomenclature may also be applied to visual disturbances associated with the perception of print and which can often be treated by use of coloured overlays or tinted lenses (see Evans 2001; Whiteley and Smith 2001). However, the label for Ewan's difficulties is much less important than what is done about them. Stuart *et al.* (2000) found that visual memory affects acquisition of sight vocabulary in young children, and this appeared to be what was happening in Ewan's case. His strengths in phonological processing and auditory working memory suggested that an immediate switch to phonically-based teaching would be beneficial, and that is what was implemented. Although progress was rather slow at first, Ewan's word recognition skills expanded significantly, and he is now (at age 10) ahead of most of his peers in reading accuracy and reading comprehension, although he still reads rather slowly and his spelling of irregular words is unreliable. At age 8, Ewan began to use a 'talking' word processor, which spoke back the text as he typed it in. Drawing on his good auditory-verbal skills, this helped Ewan to problem-solve his writing difficulties largely without teacher intervention, and to self-correct most of his errors in writing. Currently his writing is still not quite commensurate with his oral intellectual ability, but he is well on the way, and his prospects for success in secondary education are now good.

Emily, aged 12 years 2 months

Emily's father was in the Army and her family had recently moved back to the UK after several years of being stationed abroad. Emily started her education in an independent kindergarten in England, and had since attended a succession of English-speaking schools in various parts of the world. She recently joined the local comprehensive school and almost immediately the head of year identified a problem. Emily was not happy (perhaps the move had unsettled her), but also her written work and mathematics were well below that expected of her. Her previous reports suggested that she was fairly intellectually able and no early problems had been recorded. But it had been noted that she did not put a great deal of effort into her school work and so consequently her performance across most of the curriculum had been slipping for some time. She had never been assessed before and had never been provided with any additional help. It had been assumed that the problem was motivational. Emily was administered LASS Secondary, which she did not find in the least bit intimidating (in fact, she enjoyed the tests). The results are shown in Figure 4.2.

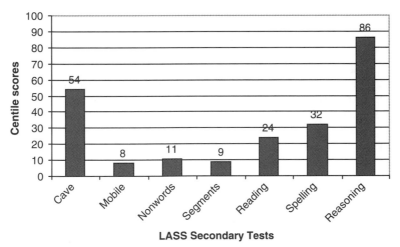

Figure 4.2 LASS Secondary results for Emily, aged 12 years 2 months.

Emily's LASS Secondary results shed a great deal of light on her problems. Space does not allow a detailed analysis of the results here, but it can be seen that, unlike Ewan, her visual memory ('Cave') was satisfactory, but her auditory working memory ('Mobile') was poor. Her Reasoning test score indicates that she was bright, but clearly under-performing in both reading and spelling. She had very limited phonic skills ('Nonwords'), which her parents later admitted could have been due to the de-emphasis on phonic teaching in her previous schools, where a 'real books' approach was in vogue. However, that is not the whole story, because she had extremely poor phonological processing ability ('Segments'), which, taken together with her poor auditory working memory and her general profile, points to a diagnosis of dyslexia. Her competence in visual memory had probably sustained her through the primary school, enabling her to rely on visual recognition of words as whole units. Her inability to tackle unfamiliar words was now letting her down in both reading and writing, especially when confronted with large numbers of subject-specific words that were new to her. The head of year decided that it would be necessary to improve Emily's phonic skills and try to increase her reading and writing abilities before she reached the start of GCSE work. A special needs teacher at the school began to help Emily work on her phonics, backed up by regular computer practice activities using the program Wordshark (Savery and Burton 1995; see also Singleton and Simmons 2001). It was also recognized that because of her weak auditory memory, she would be likely to encounter problems in revising and remembering information for examinations, so she was taught how to create mind-maps for this purpose, capitalizing on her visual memory strengths.

Emily's problems in mathematics were not so much in understanding the concepts as in remembering number facts and calculation procedures. This now made sense in the light of her LASS Secondary profile, and so her mathematics teacher created differentiated activities that gave Emily additional practice in these areas. Now, after a year in her new school, Emily's parents and teachers have noted that she has settled down and is making better progress. Her reading has improved substantially and she is now reading for pleasure, something she never did before. She is gaining confidence in her maths and in her writing, and has started to use a word processor when doing her homework. Perhaps most importantly, Emily now enjoys school and is formulating career plans that will involve going to college and so she is working hard to achieve her ambitions.

Conclusions

CBA is now a rapidly growing area in education. The two case studies reported above illustrate how CBA can assist the teacher to diagnose learning problems and develop classroom solutions for those problems. The tests employed are quick and easy to administer, produce immediate results and the children find the assessments enjoyable and stimulating. The profiles obtained can often throw up unexpected findings, as in Ewan's case, or sometimes they confirm the teacher's suspicions. In either event, the teacher has obtained solid evidence not only on which specific skills children need to acquire, but also about their learning strengths. The pattern of these underlying skills has a significant effect on learning; it is important for teachers to appreciate them and make appropriate adjustments in teaching. In some cases, a diagnostic label (such as 'dyslexia') may be helpful in promoting wider awareness of a child's problem (for example, among all teachers in the school) and in indicating the most promising educational approaches to be adopted. But this is not as important as reaching a deeper understanding of the difficulties so that appropriate strategies for learning and teaching can be implemented. Computer-based assessment appears to help teachers gain this deeper understanding and to point to key difficulties at which to direct special educational support.

References

British Psychological Society (1999) *Guidelines for the Development and Use of Computer-Based Assessments*. Leicester: BPS.

Butterworth, B. (1999) *The Mathematical Brain*. London: Macmillan.

Butterworth, B. (2001) *The Dyscalculia Screener*. Windsor: NFER-Nelson.

Crook, C. (1994) *Computers and the Collaborative Experience of Learning*. London: Routledge.

Department for Education and Skills (2001) *Special Educational Needs Code of Practice*. London: DfES.

Dillon, A. (1992) Reading from paper versus screens: a critical review of screen size and text layout on the study of text. *Behaviour and Information Technology*, 11(2): 71–8.

Drasgow, F. and Olson-Buchanan, J.B. (1999) *Innovations in Computerized Assessment*. Hillsdale, NJ: Lawrence Erlbaum Associates.

Evans, B.J.W. (2001) *Dyslexia and Vision*. London: Whurr.

Hambleton, R.K. and Swaminathan, H. (1985) *Item Response Theory: Principles and Applications*. Boston, MA: Kluwer-Nijhoff.

Horne, J.K., Singleton, C.H. and Thomas, K.V. (1999) *LASS Secondary Computerised Assessment System*. Beverley, East Yorkshire: Lucid Research.

Horne, J.K., Singleton, C.H. and Thomas, K.V. (2002a) The reliability and validity of computer-based educational tests. Unpublished manuscript, Department of Psychology, University of Hull.

Horne, J.K., Singleton, C.H. and Thomas, K.V. (2002b) Computerised screening for dyslexia in secondary education. Unpublished manuscript, Department of Psychology, University of Hull.

Horne, J.K., Singleton, C.H. and Thomas, K.V. (2002c) Gender differences in computerised educational tests. Unpublished manuscript, Department of Psychology, University of Hull.

Olsen, J.B. (1990) Applying computerized adaptive testing in schools, *Measurement and Evaluation in Counselling and Development*, 23: 31–8.

Savery, R. and Burton, R. (1995) *Wordshark*. London: Whitespace.

Singleton, C.H. (1997a) Screening early literacy, in J.R. Beech and C.H. Singleton (eds) *The Psychological Assessment of Reading*. London: Routledge.

Singleton, C.H. (1997b) Computerised assessment of reading, in J.R. Beech and C.H. Singleton (eds) *The Psychological Assessment of Reading*. London: Routledge.

Singleton, C.H. (ed.) (1999) *Dyslexia in Higher Education: Policy, Provision and Practice*. Report of the National Working Party on Dyslexia in Higher Education. Hull: University of Hull, on behalf of the Higher Education Funding Council for England.

Singleton C.H. (2001) Computer-based assessment in education, *Educational and Child Psychology*, 18(3): 58–74.

Singleton, C.H. (2002) Dyslexia: cognitive factors and implications for literacy, in G. Reid and J. Wearmouth (eds) *Dyslexia and Literacy: Theory and Practice*. London: Wiley.

Singleton, C.H. and Horne, J.K. (in press) Computerised screening for dyslexia in adults. *Journal of Research in Reading*.

Singleton, C.H. and Simmons, F.R. (2001) An evaluation of Wordshark in the classroom, *British Journal of Educational Technology*, 32(3): 317–30.

Singleton, C.H., Horne, J.K. and Vincent, D. (1995) *Implementation of a Computer-based System for the Diagnostic Assessment of Reading*. Unpublished Project Report to the National Council for Educational Technology. Hull: Department of Psychology, University of Hull.

Singleton, C.H., Thomas, K.V. and Leedale, R.C. (1996) *Lucid CoPS Cognitive Profiling System*. Beverley, East Yorkshire: Lucid Research.

Singleton, C.H., Thomas K.V. and Horne, J.K. (1998) *CoPS Baseline Assessment System*. Beverley, East Yorkshire: Lucid Research.

Singleton, C.H., Horne, J.K and Thomas K.V. (1999) Computerised baseline assessment, *Journal of Research in Reading*, 22(1): 67–80.

Singleton, C.H., Thomas K.V. and Horne, J.K. (2000) Computer-based cognitive assessment and the development of reading, *Journal of Research in Reading*, 23(2): 158–80.

Singleton, C.H., Horne, J.K. and Thomas K.V. (2002) *Lucid Adult Dyslexia Screening (LADS)*. Beverley, East Yorkshire: Lucid Research.

Snowling, M. (2000) *Dyslexia*, 2nd edn. Oxford: Blackwell.

Stuart, M., Masterson, J. and Dixon, M. (2000) Spongelike acquisition of sight vocabulary in beginning readers, *Journal of Research in Reading*, 23: 12–27.

Thomas, K.V., Singleton, C.H. and Horne, J.K. (2001) *LASS Junior Computerised Assessment System*. Beverley, East Yorkshire: Lucid Research.

Wade, B. and Moore, M. (1993) The test's the thing: viewpoints of students with special educational needs, *Educational Studies*, 19(2): 181–91.

Watkins, M.W. and Kush, J.C. (1988) Assessment of academic skills of learning disabled students with classroom microcomputers, *School Psychology Review*, 17(1): 81–8.

Whiteley, H.E. and Smith, C.D. (2001) The use of tinted lenses to alleviate reading difficulties, *Journal of Research in Reading*, 24(1): 30–40.

Wilkins, A.J. (1986) Intermittent illumination from visual display units and fluorescent lighting affects movement of eyes across text, *Human Factors*, 28: 75–81.

Wolf, M. and O'Brien, B. (2001) On issues of time, fluency and intervention, in A. Fawcett (ed.) *Dyslexia: Theory and Good Practice*. London: Whurr.

Wood, D., Underwood, J. and Avis, P. (1999) Integrated learning systems in the classroom, *Computers and Education*, 33(2/3): 91–108.

Woodward, J. and Rieth, H. (1997) A historical review of technology research in special education, *Review of Educational Research*, 67(4): 503–36.

5

INTEGRATED LEARNING SYSTEMS: EFFECTS ON LEARNING AND SELF-ESTEEM

Ian Hedley

Integrated learning systems (ILS) are controversial. Though research has failed to establish conclusively whether they have any significant effect on children's ability to read, their presence in British schools has rocketed over the last few years despite their high cost. According to a leading supplier of ILS, in 1994 just nine schools were using their system in the UK. Today, more than one in three (about 1650) schools are using ILS (RM plc 2002). Recently, the Department for Education and Employment provided the following advice:

> ILS could . . . prove a powerful tool for future classroom teachers. But design of software continues to evolve and understanding in the education system of how to use the systems effectively is still not fully developed. We do not believe that ILS should be seen as systems that offer self-contained solutions, but rather as ones that need to be carefully integrated by teachers. Whatever the potential promise of ILS may be in the medium to long term, it is important that schools look carefully at the evaluation evidence when making a commitment to this form of learning.
>
> (Department for Education and Employment 1998: §150)

The majority of schools that have invested in an ILS have done so because they see it as a way of helping pupils with weak literacy or numeracy skills. Many local education authority (LEA) services for pupils with special educational needs, such as dyslexia support and behaviour support services, have also bought ILS. This chapter looks at what ILS are and describes a case study from a secondary modern school in the south of England. It examines the research evidence about the effectiveness of ILS in teaching reading and concludes with some advice about how to make the most effective use of an ILS.

What is an integrated learning system?

Ever since Skinner (1968) described the idea of a 'teaching machine', people have been attempting to develop software that can interactively teach pupils. A teaching machine presents a pupil with some curriculum material, assesses their understanding of it and uses their responses to choose the next item. It provides instant feedback so pupils immediately know if they have responded correctly or not. This corresponded to how Skinner felt people learn, which was based on the idea that if the consequence of a behaviour or action is positive, it is likely to occur again. If there is no response or consequence, the behaviour is less likely to occur again. So in Skinner's model, people learn something new by trying it out and being positively rewarded. Modern ILS are derived from this concept and they always consist of three components (courseware, assessment and management), which together come close to Skinner's idea of an ideal teaching machine. This 'ideal' teaching machine should provide instant feedback, present work that progresses in small, always achievable steps and allow a free choice of answer. (It is this latter requirement that most ILS fail to meet.)

The courseware component of an ILS contains the curriculum material. This can be on any topic, although literacy and mathematics materials are commonly used in schools. An ILS typically has a large bank of questions that are presented in a variety of ways, limited only by the capabilities of the computer and the imagination of the developers. Thus material can be presented using animations, pictures, video or sound in addition to the usual text.

A strength of ILS is their ability to mark pupils' work 'on the fly'. When pupils answer questions, the program checks their responses and pupils know immediately if they were correct. This is the role of the assessment module (for additional information on assessment, see Chapter 4). Most ILS limit pupils' responses to multiple-choice or single-word answers as anything more complicated than this increases the likelihood that the pupil will give a correct answer that the computer does not recognize. Some ILS do allow for longer answers, but these usually have to be marked by a teacher at a later date. As well as marking work, the assessment component usually provides information to pupils and teachers about the pupils' progress over time. In many cases, this can be quite detailed and highlight strengths and weaknesses in pupils' work.

Many software packages have courseware and assessment components but what sets ILS apart is their management system. An ILS's management system takes pupils' responses and decides what the pupil should do next. This can be very sophisticated. When a pupil gets a question wrong, the system can present a similar question to check if the pupil made a simple mistake or does in fact lack understanding. If the pupil appears to lack understanding, the ILS can ask related questions to assess what it is the pupil does not understand and then present appropriate material to remedy the gap in knowledge. Sometimes an ILS will not be able to teach a particular skill and teacher intervention is required. An ILS, therefore, is most definitely not a replacement for a teacher but can move them on to different or more challenging material. The courseware material is paced according to the individual pupil needs, although most ILS will also allow the teacher to override the management system and dictate what pupils will study.

The major strengths of ILS are their ability to provide instant feedback and present work tailored to each individual pupil's needs in a way that one teacher working with a class of 30 pupils cannot do. Its principal weakness is that it is confined by the current capabilities of computer hardware and software in presenting material and recording responses.

It is important to note that there is a large (and rapidly increasing) number of ILS and they are all very different in style and effectiveness. What applies to one system need not necessarily apply to another. ILS first took off in the USA and this is evident in some products available in the UK. In some cases, passages or spellings are spoken in American accents (although the words themselves are usually British spellings) and some pupils can find this difficult to understand. A more serious concern is perhaps that American-derived ILS use American contexts and books, which may be less meaningful to British pupils. However, American ILS are usually more sophisticated, having been developed over a longer period than British systems, and are often considered effective because of the experience that has been invested in their development. Systems developed in the UK usually use book extracts that will be more familiar to British pupils and teachers and it may be easier to integrate into work that is being done in classes away from the computers. Other differences can include the kinds of tasks that are involved. Some systems, for example, have an emphasis on games and fun activities, while others take a more serious academic approach. Some pupils prefer the fun approach, while others find it patronizing.

Finally, some programs are described as ILS but they do not have the three components (courseware, assessment and management) described above (Brown 1997). Some computer programs that have a variety of different tasks and topics have been described as 'integrated' and are also 'systems for learning', but the software does not use pupils' answers to set their next tasks and so, strictly speaking, they are not integrated learning systems.

One example of an ILS is Successmaker. Successmaker consists of a central management and assessment system and a number of courses. Successmaker was originally developed in the USA but over the years has been gradually anglicized, with the latest version featuring more British accents and contexts. The courses cover mathematics, writing, spelling and reading for pupils of all ages. The spelling course uses a variety of teaching strategies and includes sound and context sentences. Pupils are taught new words of ever-increasing difficulty but are also reassessed on previously learnt vocabulary. Teachers can get a printout of words individual pupils misspelled and the mistakes they made. There are a variety of reading courses that aim to develop pupils' comprehension, vocabulary and thinking skills. The work can range from filling in a word missing from a sentence to reading a passage from a book (real books from around the world) and then doing a piece of writing on it. Some of the book passages are very rich in pictures and sound, although many of the shorter passages are presented in fairly plain text. When pupils get a question correct, they get a visual reward (a rosette) and they can check their progress at any point. This is usually very motivating for pupils. At the end of a session, pupils are told their percentage of correct questions, which is usually around 80 per cent if they have been concentrating. Teachers can view and print reports that show areas individual pupils are strong or weak in and there are often worksheets that can be printed out to support the work on the computer. Successmaker automatically selects work for pupils to do but teachers can intervene and set up specific programmes of work should they wish. The system will also warn if pupils are falling behind, so that the teacher can intervene.

Implementing an ILS at Carter Community Sports College

Carter Community Sports College is a secondary modern school serving a relatively deprived area of an otherwise affluent town. Of the approximately 120 new pupils arriving at the school each year in Year 8 (aged 12), between 15 and 35 per cent usually have reading ages 3 or more years behind their chronological ages. The school invested in an ILS (Successmaker) to work with these large numbers of pupils in an effective but affordable way. A learning support assistant is employed to work with pupils while they are using Successmaker and to manage the system day-to-day.

The school has experimented with a variety of different ways of time-tabling pupils on the ILS. Initially, pupils came out of their usual lessons for half an hour at the same time each day, five days a week. They used courseware covering reading, spelling and mathematics as recommended by the providers of the system. Under this condition, pupils made very good progress when compared with a control group. Unfortunately, half-hour slots did not correspond very well with 50-minute lessons and pupils' work in curriculum subjects suffered, as they were often missing parts of two different subjects each day. The timetabling was changed so that pupils went on the ILS for 20 minutes a time (doing the reading and spelling modules), four days a week. This meant they missed just half of one lesson in four different subjects each week. For pupils in the lower ability sets, the mathematics work was incorporated into mathematics lessons. This new implementation had less of an impact on pupils' work in curriculum lessons and they still made good progress with their reading. Some of the pupils found coming out of lessons at different times each day confusing, and they often missed sessions. This was not always due to forgetfulness; some pupils just did not like missing their lessons to use it.

A teacher was in charge of monitoring pupils' use of the system, although the learning support assistant involved usually intervened and organized alternative work when necessary. The teacher did not usually work directly with the pupils and it was felt that perhaps the ILS would be more effective if it could be integrated more closely with work in English lessons. This would enable English teachers to use information provided by the Successmaker's reporting system to inform their teaching and monitor the progress of pupils working through the courseware. As a result, pupils currently use the ILS four times a week, for 20 minutes, but two of these sessions take place during English lessons. English teachers take an active role in monitoring and intervening with pupils and this is leading to more substantial progress for a greater number of pupils. Pupils have breaks, spending no more than one term on the system, then having one term off.

Integrated learning systems for developing literacy skills

To monitor Successmaker's effectiveness, pupils at Carter Community Sports College are assessed using a paper-based group reading test once or twice a year. It is important to use a separate test rather than rely on Successmaker's internal reporting system. If the ILS is not managed effectively and no teacher intervention takes place, the pupil can progress to more and more difficult work without any understanding. The pupil will appear to make progress if only the crude levels reported by the ILS are examined. This is because if the system cannot teach a pupil a skill even after remediation, it will alert the teacher but then automatically move the pupil onto the next level. As a result, research that relies on the reporting systems of an ILS (Becker, cited in McFarlane 1997; Brooks *et al.* 1998) provides information about the individual pupil's progress through the courseware and little about the quality of their learning.

There does not seem to be any way to predict how well pupils are going to do before putting them on the system. Some pupils just do not enjoy or learn from the ILS we use at Carter Community Sports College. There are several possible reasons for this. For example, the courseware does attempt to use interesting passages, but these are not matched to pupils' interests in any way, so there is no guarantee that the pupils themselves will find them motivating. Similarly, there is no attempt to match the delivery of the content to pupils' learning styles. Instead, a variety of presentations are used in the hope that at least some of them will match pupils' preferred learning styles. Although material can be presented in ways appropriate to a wide range of learning styles, there is no getting away from the fact that pupils have to sit at a computer and look at a screen. This does not suit everyone. It is important to remember that ILS are derived primarily from Skinner's concept of a teaching machine and as Drummond (quoted in Bonnett 1997: 157) says, 'Because children's behaviour and children's learning is so various and complex, it is highly unlikely that any one simple framework of understanding, any single model of learning, will give us the "position" from which we will be able to understand every-thing we see'. Whitehead (1989) further warns that the process of learning to read is complicated and sophisticated and we must be careful of 'cen-tralised, simplistic and inappropriate interventions in the curriculum' (p. 135), an accusation that is often levelled at ILS.

There is also an issue with how most ILS accept answers. For the software to be able to mark work, it is often very strict about how it allows pupils to answer questions, making it frustrating for (often very able) pupils who have their own preferred and effective methods (Parr 1995). This is more of an issue with mathematics than reading courses. Many reading courses allow pupils to write longer answers, but these then have to be marked by a teacher, which effectively stops the system being an ILS in the proper sense of the term.

Research has also been quite vague about who benefits most from using an ILS, although perhaps unsurprisingly, those with the lowest starting point usually make least progress (Underwood *et al.* 1996). However, when compared with a control group of similar pupils who have not used an ILS, pupils of high and low ability using an ILS have been found to make large *comparative* gains, whereas those of average ability have not appeared to gain any additional benefits from time on such systems (McFarlane 1997). What we have found at Carter Community Sports College is that pupils who begin with very low reading ages (usually below 7 years) need add-itional teaching, away from the computer, if they are to make significant progress, but that the vast majority of pupils, although initially still behind with their reading, do make excellent progress.

Despite the high numbers of pupils arriving at the school in Year 8 with reading ages below 9.5 years (including some below 7), in the first two year groups to have been exposed to an ILS from their arrival at the school until leaving four years later, only one pupil in each year has left with a reading age below 10. Average gains in reading ages for year groups at Carter Community Sports College have ranged from almost zero in one case to over 3 years in another. Usually year groups have gained an average of about a year and a half in reading age over a period of one chronological year, from well below average starting points. Some pupils do significantly better than others, while some pupils do not benefit from using the ILS at all. For these pupils, the school has alternative provision, such as paired-reading or specialist literacy teaching.

Although we have found that using Successmaker has improved the reading ability of most pupils at the school, the published research evidence for the impact of ILS on reading suggests a more equivocal finding. For example, Becker (1992) found that ' ILS have not achieved their potential in American education. Their use does not appear to be consistently raising measured pupil achievement in reading ... as might be expected from pupils using high quality software throughout the year'.

Part of the problem with published research, according to Kenny (1998), is that it often looks at a variety of different systems and then aggregates the results (for example, National Council for Educational Technology 1994, 1996; Becta 1998). This is less than ideal because the systems do not form a homogeneous group (Brown 1997). When individual systems are examined, significant gains in reading ability are often but not always found (Parr 1995; Fitzgerald *et al.* 1996; Underwood *et al.* 1996). A 1998 British Educational Communications and Technology Agency (Becta) report did not find any significant gains for reading when averaged over all the ILS it studied but, although it was not published in the actual report, some individual systems came out more positively than others when looked at on their own (John 1997).

What has been difficult to measure at Carter Community Sports College has been the impact of Successmaker on pupils' progress in curriculum subjects. The introduction of the ILS corresponded with many other initiatives, which together have seen GCSE results at the school improve tremendously. How much of this has been due to the ILS itself is impossible to say. In fact, there is no strong research evidence of pupils generalizing what they learn on an ILS (Parr 1995; McFarlane 1997; Becta 1998), perhaps because of its narrow model of teaching (McFarlane 1997) and the fact that it often teaches new skills out of any meaningful contexts (Parr 1995). There is also concern that ILS teach pupils 'procedural rather than strategic rules' (Lewis 1997: 117), which might result in making the transfer of skills into different contexts more difficult. On top of all this, pupils often have to miss their normal lessons to use the software. Some research has found that pupils using an ILS do worse in their GCSEs than might be expected (Becta 1998).

At Carter Community Sports College, most teachers and pupils have said they feel the time spent on the ILS has been worthwhile and justifies the missing of some curriculum time. Two OFSTED inspections of the school (while acknowledging the adverse effect missing parts of lessons can have on pupils' progress in those particular subjects) have come to the same conclusion. Both teachers and pupils at Carter Community Sports College are positive about the software, although teachers have found it difficult to identify any objective evidence from their lessons about how pupils were benefiting, other than changes in behaviour that might suggest improved self-esteem. This has been replicated in other research, where teachers have been found to be enthusiastic about ILS (Fitzgerald *et al.* 1996; National Council for Educational Technology 1996) without necessarily having any objective evidence to justify such confidence (Becta 1998). Pupils at Carter Community Sports College, however, have commented that 'I can read more better now', 'Made me think harder' and 'I can read better, like longer'.

Yet not all comments have been positive, with one pupil saying, 'Can't concentrate on it. Winds me up when I'm on the computer with it. Gives me a headache. And I don't like reading at all anyway'. Also, a teacher at the school has said that:

> I can actually say in some cases . . . that I've actually seen no improvement whatever and actually [one pupil has] gone backwards . . . I get the feeling with [this system] that it's very low level and it doesn't necessarily stretch the pupil to beyond, you know it works within its comfort zone . . . What you may be gaining in the ILS, depending how it's run, you may actually be losing something else in another area.

Pupils at Carter Community Sports College tend to become less enthusiastic about the ILS the longer they use it. In some cases, this is because the initial enjoyment of using computers can wear off in time (Cavendish *et al.* 1997; Becker, quoted in McFarlane 1997). In other cases, pupils become weary of the repetitive nature of the system's work. It is for this reason pupils have regular breaks – usually one term on, one term off. By the time pupils get to Year 10, when in some instances they have been using the ILS for two years, they have usually had enough. Although this applies to very few pupils (as most have made enough progress to stop using the system by then), the school is currently investigating alternative provision for Years 10 and 11.

To summarize the above, at Carter Community Sports College we have found that most pupils improve their reading by using the ILS we have invested in. In common with published research, we have been unable to predict in advance which pupils will or will not benefit from time on the system. We have found that pupils who use the system for too long (more than two terms in any one year, or more than two years) quite often stop enjoying it, even though they were initially very enthusiastic. Pupils who do enjoy using the ILS tend to be the ones who make most progress. It is very difficult to say how much of an impact using an ILS has had on pupils' learning in other subjects, but the system's introduction, together with many other whole-school initiatives, has corresponded with the school's best ever GCSE results.

Integrated learning systems and self-esteem

Self-esteem is important in education because self-esteem and academic success usually go hand-in-hand (Purkey 1970; Lawrence 1996). For most people, this relationship is reciprocal – success increases self-esteem and increased self-esteem leads to success:

> Those doing well will not only internalise a positive view of themselves but also enjoy more satisfactory relationships with peers, teachers and parents as a result of their success. This, in turn, increases the child's motivation to approach academic tasks with confidence and persistence. In such a way, then, self-concept can become a predictor of academic performance.
>
> (Burns 1982: 215)

However, work conducted by Lawrence (1996) and Coopersmith (cited in Gurney 1988) has portrayed self-esteem as a 'threshold' variable. Pupils with low self-esteem tend to withdraw effort either because they fear failure if they attempt a task or because they need to avoid situations that might alter their ideas about themselves (Burns 1982; Gurney 1988; Thompson 1993; Lawrence 1996). Burns (1982) cited work by Brookover, Erikson and Joiner (from 1967) that found that positive self-esteem was necessary, but not sufficient, for academic achievement. So for people with very low self-esteem, 'it is not possible to help the pupil achieve success with a skill approach until he/she has had a change of self-concept' (Lawrence 1996: 75).

Because of the close link with achievement, many pupils with special educational needs have low self-esteem. For many, academic progress is likely to continue to be slow until their self-esteem is improved. This can be particularly hard to do in school for low-achieving pupils, as school could well be seen by them as a place of failure. Using an ILS is one method that can help redress this, as it provides instant and continuous feedback that is overwhelmingly positive, with a built-in success level in many systems of around 80 per cent. This instant feedback is appreciated by both teachers and pupils (National Council for Educational Technology 1994; Fitzgerald *et al.* 1996; Cavendish *et al.* 1997; McFarlane 1997), perhaps because praise from a computer may seem to many pupils to be more objective and, therefore, more believable than that from an adult. Pupils at Carter Community Sports College have said it does not matter if you get a question wrong on the computer because 'no-one knows' and it is easy to correct without making work look untidy.

Success on an ILS can help pupils begin to think of themselves as people who can learn. There is clearer evidence about the effect on pupils' self-esteem when using an ILS than there is about its effect on literacy skills. Pupils using an ILS have been found to become more confident about their ability and to have increased academic self-esteem (Parr 1995; Cavendish *et al.* 1997). These same studies have found that pupils using an ILS become less dependent on the classroom teacher. This increase in self-esteem is often one of the first things teachers notice, long before any obvious improvement in pupils' literacy skills. Teachers at Carter Community Sports College have noticed that pupils using the ILS have been more willing to ask for help, have tried harder in class and have focused more on their work. One teacher said, 'I have noticed a difference in attitude, they tend to be more settled and attentive . . . more confident and seemingly more part of the class'. Another said, 'Confidence to me is the first thing I noticed. The kids were much happier to actually write'. Most pupils when asked have said they felt their reading had got better, although not all have attributed this to using the ILS.

Integrated learning systems and collaborative learning

A strength of the ILS approach is the system's ability to match the course-ware material to each individual pupil's progress (Becker 1992; Fitzgerald *et al.* 1996; McFarlane, cited in Lewis 1997). In theory, a computer can do this better than any teacher could ever do in a class, although there is some evidence that some systems move pupils along too slowly or, less commonly, too quickly (National Council for Educational Technology 1994; Parr 1995; Hativa, cited in McFarlane 1997). Putting pupils to work in pairs on an ILS should not be effective, as it would interfere with the computer's ability to match the work to the pupil. In practice, however, there is evidence to suggest that pairs working collaboratively may lead to increased gains in reading and to greater boosts in self-esteem.

Becker (1992) felt that combining cooperative learning methods with an ILS might make the software more effective and in 1997 Brush (1997a) conducted a study which investigated this idea. He placed pupils in pairs, matched by ability, on the mathematics module of an ILS. He argued that this would address some of the concerns expressed by many about ILS – pupils would not be working for long periods in isolation and more pupils would be able to access the system, making it more cost-effective. Brush found that pupils who had been working in cooperative pairs did significantly better than those who had been working through the same material on their own. He also found that the pupils who had been working in pairs were more positive about the subject (mathematics) and the ILS itself. He suggested that this might be because pupils working together could assist each other and provide alternative approaches to solving the problems presented and that pupils working in pairs spent more time on the task than those working on their own. He also thought that teachers were able to provide more effective assistance to those pupils who were working in pairs. Brush suggested that feeling isolated when working on the system contributed to more negative thoughts about both the subject and the software. He also found that 'the relationship between the group and preference for working with a partner was not significant' (Brush 1997a: 62), but that more individuals than pairs expressed a preference for working with a partner. These results were very interesting but, as Brush himself cautioned, it is dangerous to generalize. Only one system was examined, using only one course on that system, and only one group of pupils.

In a separate study, Brush (1997b) looked at the effects of grouping pupils heterogeneously (high-ability paired with low-ability) rather than homogeneously. He found the kind of grouping had little effect on achievement outcomes, but that pupils working in heterogeneous pairs spent more time on the task than those pupils who were in a homogeneous pair. As Clariana (1997) noted, this should translate into increased learning.

At Carter Community Sports College, we conducted our own project to see how pupils would perform if they worked on the system in pairs rather than as individuals. Pupils of roughly equal reading ability were put into groups of four and from each group two were randomly selected to work together and two were left to work as individuals. Pupils were given paper-based reading tests at the start of the project and at the end, six months later. Those who worked in a pair did at least as well as those who worked on their own and often better, although in some cases one half of a pair made significantly more progress than the other. The paired pupils were generally more positive about their reading than the individuals. The self-esteem of all pupils was, on average, improved, more so for those who had worked with a partner. Where there were problems, it was with pupils not liking their partner and therefore not wanting to work with them, or with the learning support assistant having to work with larger numbers of pupils than usual because of the greater number of pupils being able to use the system at the same time.

Eleven pupils were interviewed as part of the project. One pair that met with mixed success was Jenny and Kelly (pupils' names have been changed). Jenny's reading age increased by 1.5 years over the 6-month period but Kelly's fell back 0.13 years. Kelly complained of headaches because the screen was too bright. Jenny did not feel she had worked well with Kelly 'cos we don't work good as a team . . . we're always arguing over the [answers]'. She preferred working on her own 'because I don't like sharing'. This was how she worked in class too. The worst thing about working with someone else, according to Jenny, was that 'you had to keep moving the keyboards around'. Kelly usually did all the reading and Jenny the spellings and they helped each other if one got stuck. When Kelly was doing the reading Jenny 'got bored, started shouting at her'. In future she would prefer to work on her own. 'It would help a lot more because I'm studying a lot more on my own'. However, one pupil who was part of a pair where both made good progress gave examples of the advantages of having a partner: 'Well she asks me for help more . . . I think she struggles a bit on it. Cos like, say like if there's a word, like quacking or something like that, she'll say oh how do you spell that and I'll say you try and say it first and I'll help you if it's not it'.

Disadvantages of integrated learning systems

There is no doubt that ILS are expensive to buy and set up. They do not run themselves and so ongoing monitoring and systems for intervention are necessary. This adds to the cost still further. The ILS method of teaching does not suit all pupils – some pupils do not like it and others do not learn from it. Schools must not rely on investment in an ILS to solve all their pupils' learning difficulties. The amount of time available in a school day is limited and if pupils are spending time on an ILS they will not be spending time learning anything else, so before placing any pupils on such a system the teacher must be sure that it will be a good use of their time. Unfortunately, because there is no evidence that enables teachers to predict if an individual pupil will learn from an ILS, there is no way of knowing in advance if it *will* be a good use of an individual's time. Comparative research (Brooks *et al.* 1998) has suggested that with respect to literacy, other reading intervention schemes may be more effective than an ILS.

Benefits of integrated learning systems

Case studies have shown that many pupils do benefit from working on an ILS and some pupils make spectacular progress with their reading and spelling skills. Many pupils really enjoy using an ILS and the majority become more confident as a result of using one. Although the initial financial outlay can be considerable and there are running costs, the cost per pupil per year (in terms of money and teaching time), once the system is in place, is significantly lower than it is with most other reading intervention schemes. Where schools have large numbers of pupils who have significant difficulties, an ILS can be a useful support to teacher-led interventions.

Implications for teachers

Given the high percentage of schools currently using ILS, most teachers will at some stage in their career work with pupils who are following such a course. It may be that they find their pupils leaving their lessons to go to an ILS session, in which case some understanding of why it is necessary for pupils to attend such sessions (to get their four or more sessions a week) may be all that is required. However, ILS can provide rich information about pupils' strengths and weaknesses that all teachers can make use of in their planning. This could be of particular (although by no means exclusive) benefit to beginning teachers, who may not yet have developed the same skills in identifying strengths and weaknesses in pupils as their more experienced colleagues.

In some cases, teachers may find themselves responsible for managing a group of pupils' access to and progress on an ILS. This is a task often given to relatively newly qualified teachers who are seen as more skilled in all things connected with computers! It must be remembered that an ILS is not about using a computer but about learning and, as this chapter set out to show, great thought needs to go into making it work. All teachers finding themselves involved in using an ILS should therefore be aware of how to make the most of such an expensive piece of software.

Conclusions

An ILS can be a huge investment for a school, at least initially, and it is important that everything possible is done to make sure the system is effective. How an ILS is implemented can be every bit as important to its effectiveness as the quality of the system itself (Van Dusen and Worthen 1992; Parr 1995; National Council for Educational Technology 1996; Becta 1998). Pupils need access to the system for frequent but short periods of time. For pupils with special educational needs, 10 minutes may be long enough; for other pupils, 30 minutes per session is an absolute maximum. Ideally, pupils should use an ILS once a day, although this can vary according to the particular system. Certainly if it is used for less than three sessions a week it is usually ineffective. This amount of use has implications for timetabling, especially in secondary schools. Use of the system can be integrated into lessons – for example, as part of English lessons – pupils can be withdrawn from lessons or there can be a combination of withdrawal and integration.

The management system of an ILS makes decisions about the next piece of work pupils will do every time they answer a question, but it cannot be left entirely to itself (McFarlane 1997). Someone (a teacher or teaching assistant) must examine the reports the assessment component produces and check to see if intervention is necessary. This intervention can range from adjusting the ILS itself (perhaps lowering a pupil's level) to taking the pupil off the system to work in some other way for a while. Some systems can generate worksheets that can be completed away from the computer, with help if appropriate. What is very important, however, is that someone is checking to make sure pupils are not simply left to do harder and harder work with less and less understanding.

As there is no clear evidence about how to guarantee an ILS will work, it is very important to continually monitor its effectiveness. This monitoring should not rely on data generated by the ILS itself but on independent assessments. Where pupils are using the system to improve their literacy skills, paper-based reading and spelling tests can be used to track progress. The results can then be monitored and changes made to the implementation if it is not working.

Putting pupils to work together in pairs may well increase the effectiveness of an integrated learning system. This method also increases the cost-effectiveness of the system, as many more pupils are able to use it. However, pairs must want to work together for an extended period of time.

Many pupils benefit from time on an ILS. A significant minority of pupils do not. An ILS can form a central part of a school's special educational needs provision, but it should always be just that, a part of a wider set of resources, that is continuously being evaluated and developed.

References

Becker, H.J. (1992) A model for improving the performance of integrated learning systems, *Educational Technology*, September, pp. 6–15.

Bonnett, M. (1997) Computers in the classroom: some values issues, in A. McFarlane (ed.) *Information Technology and Authentic Learning*. London: Routledge.

British Educational Communications and Technology Agency (1998) *The UK ILS Evaluations: Final Report*. Coventry: Becta.

Brooks, G., Flanagan, N., Henkhuzens, Z. and Hutchison, D. (1998) *What Works for Slow Readers?* Slough: National Foundation for Educational Research.

Brown, J. (1997) When is a system an ILS?, in J. Underwood and J. Brown (eds) *Integrated Learning Systems: Potential into Practice*. Oxford: Heinemann/NCET.

Brush, T.A. (1997a) The effects on student achievement and attitudes when using integrated learning systems with cooperative pairs, *Educational Technology Research and Development*, 45(1): 51–64.

Brush, T.A. (1997b) The effects of group composition on achievement and time on task for students completing ILS activities in co-operative pairs, *Journal of Research on Computing in Education*, 30(1): 2–17.

Burns, R. (1982) *Self-Concept Development and Education*. London: Holt, Rinehart & Winston.

Cavendish, S., Underwood, J., Lawson, T. and Dowling, S. (1997) When and why do pupils learn from ILS?, in J. Underwood and J. Brown (eds) *Integrated Learning Systems: Potential into Practice*. Oxford: Heinemann/NCET.

Clariana, R. (1997) Pace in mastery-based computer-assisted learning, *British Journal of Educational Technology*, 28(2): 135–7.

Department for Education and Employment (1998) *The Implementation of the Numeracy Strategy* (http://www.dfes.gov.uk/numeracy/chapter3.shtml).

Fitzgerald, D., Hughes, P. and Fitzgerald, R.N. (1996) *An Evaluation of Computer Assisted Learning in Victorian Schools* (www.softweb.vic.edu.au/lt/cal_eval.htm): accessed November 1998.

Gurney, P.W. (1988) *Self-Esteem in Children with Special Educational Needs*. London: Routledge.

John, M. (1997) Technology head resigns, *Times Educational Supplement*, 17 January (www.tes.co.uk): accessed October 1999.

Kenny, J. (1998) Jury still out on the success builders, *Times Educational Supplement*, 10 July (www.tes.co.uk): accessed October 1999.

Lawrence, D. (1996) *Enhancing Self-Esteem in the Classroom*. London: Paul Chapman.

Lewis, A. (1997) Integrated learning systems and pupils with special educational needs, in J. Underwood and J. Brown (eds) *Integrated Learning Systems: Potential into Practice*. Oxford: Heinemann/NCET.

McFarlane, A. (1997) The effectiveness of ILS, in J. Underwood and J. Brown (eds) *Integrated Learning Systems: Potential into Practice*. Oxford: Heinemann/NCET.

National Council for Educational Technology (1994) *ILS: Integrated Learning Systems. A Report of the Pilot Evaluation of ILS in the UK*. Coventry: NCET.

National Council for Educational Technology (1996) *ILS: Integrated Learning Systems. A Report of Phase II of the Pilot Evaluation of ILS in the UK*. Coventry: NCET.

Parr, J.M. (1995) How successful is 'Successmaker'?: issues arising from an evaluation of computer assisted learning in a secondary school, *Australian Journal of Educational Technology*, 11(1): 20–7.

Purkey, W.W. (1970) *Self-Concept and School Achievement*. New York: Prentice-Hall.

RM plc (2002) *Facts and Figures* (www.rm.com/Company/Generic.ASP?cref=GP1603): accessed May 2002.

Skinner, B.F. (1968) *The Technology of Teaching*. Englewood Cliffs, NJ: Prentice-Hall.

Thompson, T. (1993) Characteristics of self-worth protection in achievement behaviour, *British Journal of Educational Psychology*, 63: 469–88.

Underwood, J., Cavendish, S., Dowling, S., Fogelman, K. and Lawson, T. (1996) Are integrated learning systems effective learning support tools? *Computers and Education*, 26(1–3): 33–40.

Van Dusen, L.M. and Worthen, B.R. (1992) Factors that facilitate or impede implementation of integrated learning systems, *Educational Technology*, September, pp. 16–22.

Whitehead, M. (1989) Reading – caught or taught? Some issues involved in changed approaches to the teaching of reading, in P. Murphy and B. Moon (eds) *Developments in Learning and Assessment*. London: Hodder & Stoughton.

6

A WHOLE-SCHOOL APPROACH TO ICT FOR CHILDREN WITH PHYSICAL DISABILITIES

Clive Lilley

Doretta presented as a smiling, affable and gregarious 11-year-old girl to the new, young teacher who walked into her classroom in September 1974. She had cerebral palsy with quadriplegia and athetosis and was going to be a challenge to a teacher who had had no experience of pupils with a physical difficulty. A brief period of observation indicated that her academic development was being seriously hampered by her inability to record any work. Not only was her gross and fine motor control limited, but she also had no expressive language. Discussion with her physio-therapist resulted in, what was at that time, a revolutionary idea of her attempting to use an electric typewriter as the main way of recording work. Athetoid movement made it extremely difficult for her to use the correct keys and so lead weights were strapped to her wrists to try and limit some of the involuntary movement. What resulted was a slow and labori-ous process dogged by enormous inaccuracy. It was far from the ideal solution, but it allowed her to record her work in a way never before pos-sible. Even more important, it gave her a means of expressing herself in written language. Doretta's experience showed that technology was likely to provide part of the solution for pupils with physical difficulties to access education and to have an alternative means of communication. And the effect this had on the teacher? It made me appreciate the potential for technology and made me determined to encourage and make use of whatever technological innovations came along.

The rapid technological developments in the years following my work with Doretta and her physiotherapist reinforced my belief in the importance of technology. Microcomputers appeared: our school, for example, was given the same machines as local secondary schools. Their use initially was limited, since there were few of the input devices and special software now widely available. The arrival of the BBC microcomputer changed everything, simply because of the innovative software and special access devices that began to be available for it. This chapter considers the impact of information and communications technology (ICT), during the past 14 years, on one school for children with physical difficulties. This impact has been on the whole school and we have needed to take a 'whole-school' approach to ensure team working and the maximum possible benefit for all children. This has had many benefits – indeed, the school now has 'Beacon School' status – not least in leading to an increasing outreach role for the school's experience in using ICT. The much-vaunted term 'inclusion' has taken on a new meaning, as school staff increasingly help mainstream colleagues to understand the ways in which ICT can support children with special needs in mainstream classrooms.

ICT and the Blackfriars School mission

Blackfriars School is an all-age, co-educational, day special school for 180 children who have physical and medical difficulties, some of whom may have associated moderate or severe learning difficulties, sensory impairment and epilepsy. A large professional team supports them. It comprises teachers, teaching assistants, physiotherapists, speech and language therapists, medical, social and voluntary agencies, and support and ancillary staff. The team works hard to fulfil the mission statement: 'A school where intellectual independence, physical independence and social independence can flourish'. Information and communication technology plays a fundamental part in achieving this mission. It does this in two main ways: by having control over one's own means of communication and being able to record work independently.

The first is arguably the more important. The ICT coordinator at Blackfriars School believes that communication *through whatever means* is the key issue. The coordinator would prefer to change the title to 'communicating information through technology' (CIT rather than ICT), which more accurately reflects the emphasis within the school. Her view is that the key aim of the school is to enable pupils to have control over their way of communicating, whether through the use of computer, communication device or any other means, and that this must be available, quickly, immediately, consistently and reliably. The implication is that a range of both high-technology and low-technology aids need to be available.

Controversy can often surround this decision as some people, particularly parents, think that a very expensive piece of high-technology equipment will be the answer to all communication needs. The ICT coordinator reported on a discussion that took place at a Computers and Multiple Impairments Network Meeting on the difficulties faced by non-speaking pupils with very little motor control, who were assessed for multi-level communication aids. These are electronic aids, which 'speak' words, phrases and sentences when a key is pressed. They are 'multi-level' in the number of choices they offer to the user. Since the number of keys on the key pad is limited, it is usual to program them in layers, to give more choice of utterances. Apart from the time needed to customize and learn how to use these devices, the pupils are expected to be able to use complex scanning skills to make a selection from a page of words or symbols in order to communicate. The consensus reached at the meeting was that there is no sense in giving a pupil a complicated, multi-level scanning device to ask for a drink and to find a page with the correct symbol when it is far simpler and easier for them to indicate their need by eye pointing.

The simple message to be grasped from this example is that, although hi-tech aids are important, and have a vital and central role in helping children to communicate, they should not be the inevitable choice when a low-tech aid may be cheaper, quicker, more effective and efficient. When looking at the needs of individual pupils, it is necessary to adopt the holistic approach and so to devise an individual package that is uniquely appropriate for the specific pupil.

Assessing children for their assistive technology requirements

It is important that pupils are assessed regularly for any assistive technology requirements that they might have and that they are provided with the most appropriate equipment to meet their needs. Assessments commence as soon as a pupil enters Blackfriars School and an individual programme is provided for each pupil. Figure 6.1 is an example of the initial assessment when Tom entered the school. This programme is regularly monitored and updated with reference made to positioning, peripherals, software and targets to ensure a consistent approach. It is vital that everybody working with the pupil is fully conversant with the individual programme and all conform towards the same aim.

A second example is Samantha, who is 13 years old and has cerebral palsy. She is functioning academically at her chronological age but has no expressive language and has poor fine and gross motor control. The aim of the following individual programme, which is being used now for

Name Tom	*Date* Sept 2002	*Class* 7+
Age 11	*Teacher* AW	

Equipment used

E.g. Seating/Position   wheelchair

Sensory Needs/Communication

Will follow an object making a sound, eye pointing to indicate which direction he wants the object to go

---

Access Needs

Moves both arms. Switch is attached to wheelchair on right hand side. Thomas hits switch with his elbow – very slight movement.

Targets/Aims

Long Term

♦   Permanent position for switch

♦   Scanning

♦   Use left hand for another switch

Short Term

♦   Establish reliable switch position

♦   Experiential reaction to activity on computer screen

♦   Experiential reaction to sound from computer

♦   Cause and effect on computer

♦   Switch building

♦   Timed activation

Suggested Software	*Other Activities*
♦ SENSwitcher	♦ Powerlink – cause and effect, timed reaction – cassette player, fan, video, toys
♦ Ameba	
♦ Splatter	♦ Press & Hold – Powerlink, Remote control car
♦ Touch Games	
♦ Build	
♦ Switch On – Build + Reaction Timing	

Figure 6.1   Example of an ICT needs/initial assessment for Tom.

Samantha, is to give Samantha more independence to work on the computer:

- An ultra-compact keyboard with guard and a gated joystick allows her to move the cursor on the screen.
- A large 'jelly-bean' switch replaces the left-click function on a normal mouse.
- All the above are linked to a Mouser 3. The Mouser links a normal mouse plus a joystick (or other device). It is a device that connects between the mouse and the computer to allow switches to be used instead of the mouse buttons. It can turn off unwanted mouse buttons to avoid unplanned presses bringing up unwanted menus. It allows any or all of the standard mouse buttons to be turned off. It also allows switch access to these buttons for young disabled users.

Ann is 11 years old and is severely disabled after a road traffic accident. She is confined to a wheelchair and requires access to ICT to enable her to communicate and function alongside her peers. She has lost her expressive language and has limited motor control of her limbs. Her access to recorded work had to start from scratch when she joined the school and the most obvious solution was through a switch using the thumb of her right hand. A jelly-bean switch was set into a specially adapted tray that fitted on to her wheelchair. To practise her switch technique, she was encouraged to use a range of software programs that are conventionally described as 'cause and effect' and 'building' programs. The aim of these is that switch operation by a child causes interesting things to happen on the computer screen. The child comes to gain greater control of switch use and increased understanding of how he or she can influence events on the computer.

Two years later, Ann has developed some speech and is now working on simple scanning software (Clicker 4 – a widely-used piece of software that allows children to click on pictures and phrases which the computer can speak if desired) that can easily be customized. She has developed and changed her switch technique and is more confident to work in less familiar situations, where the switch may be attached on a new piece of equipment in a different place (for example, a switch on a universal mount attached to her standing frame).

Regular monitoring is vital, as needs change and pupils may outgrow what has initially been provided for them. This has proved to be easier within the primary department as the pupils are classroom-based, with one teacher and two teaching assistants. The routine in the secondary department is completely different and based on a mainstream model with pupils changing rooms for specific subjects. They also work with up to 14 different teachers for the varying subjects, with only the teaching assistant remaining constant. There is the pressure to get to lessons on time, to commence work immediately and to complete it in a given time.

Although this makes the implementation of the ICT programme logistically very difficult, it is important that the secondary department should be organized in this way, particularly for those pupils whom we are trying to re-integrate into the mainstream sector.

Current issues for schools using ICT

Switch users

Switches are a valuable means to access the school and home environment. Apart from being connected to a computer, they can be attached to battery-operated devices with a battery adapter. An AbleNet Powerlink will enable a switch to operate any mains appliance. The Mouser enables many more pupils to interact with any software. Therefore, pupils with more complex needs at Blackfriars School who are not class-based can have more opportunities to access the curriculum. It is important that providing control should be in effect from the early years of a child's life. Within the early years group, an emphasis is placed on the use of switch-controlled toys. The sensory room was designed to enable the pupils to control their environment and to understand more clearly 'cause and effect'. This room has become central to much of the work undertaken with the younger children and has proved to be extremely motivating.

> People with physical and sensory disabilities have decreased opportunities to establish contingency awareness. When contingency awareness is not established the individual does not learn that he or she can control the environment or the behaviour of others. The individual may become passive and be at risk for developing learned helplessness.
>
> (ACE Centre 2000: 1)

Nevertheless, it remains the case that those children who solely use a switch can only work for limited periods and rely heavily on staff support. Despite the number of software applications that are suitable for switch input, this remains a difficult and complex access method. It is to be hoped that technological advances in the future will find new ways for these children to access software quickly.

Portable word processors

Portable word processors (not laptop computers) are a simple solution for recording but lack the sophistication of being able to edit and present work. For many pupils, just to complete work faster is a great achievement and for this the Alphasmart 3000 is particularly impressive. It is very portable, stores 64 pages of text and can download into any word-processing program where it can be edited and printed. Several of the pupils have the benefit of a dedicated laptop. These give independence in all subject areas but in some cases have had to have adaptations made and appropriate peripherals provided. In addition, assistance is required in transporting them around school and ensuring that they are 'set up' in the correct way at the right time in the right place.

Working at speed

The problem for many pupils is that of speed. Pupils who have physical problems without any cognitive difficulties are usually those with cerebral palsy, neuromuscular problems or dyspraxia. They can move the cursor with a mouse, trackerball or rollerball but cannot always make a selection, because in trying to access the select button they can accidentally move the ball/joystick or mouse.

Expectations placed on children

As with all our pupils, the academic expectations in school are high. Staff and most parents of the higher ability pupils expect comparable results to mainstream pupils and the majority in this category follow GCSE or Entry Level courses. Presentation of work is highly important and the computer software used is complex and demanding. In ICT classes, senior groups are taught Microsoft Excel, Powerpoint and Publisher and do complicated searches on the Internet. All pupils enter externally accredited ICT examinations.

Mixed disability groups

Teaching groups of up to 12 pupils with mixed disabilities is a demanding and challenging task. In Year 10, for example, there are two pupils with arthrogryposis, two with neuromuscular disabilities, several with varying levels of cerebral palsy and two with spina bifida. One particular pupil needs extensive equipment to access the curriculum. He has cerebral palsy and can communicate very well using a communication card. He requires a portable device with peripherals and a system was customized in the ICT suite. Typing can be accomplished by the aid of a keyguard and he can move the mouse with a joystick. However, he has to rely on staff help at all times because of his inability to target the small icons using complex software such as Excel, even when things have been enlarged. A solution and a saviour to the teacher arrived in the form of Mouser 3 (described earlier). This:

• Allows a switch to be used as a select mechanism while allowing another device such as a trackerball or joystick to be used alongside a mouse.

- Provides independence and the ability to work faster.
- Allows intervention from staff to use the mouse. (This has been useful in allowing a pupil to 'catch up' or to provide assistance when errors are made and is excellent for group work. This is particularly so when working with groups of pupils with more complex physical and learning difficulties, who often do group work sitting around a projector and screen or whiteboard. The cursor can be placed on an object and the pupil can make the selection.)
- Enables two pupils to work together.
- Means that two switches can be used at the same time (useful for various applications such as to replace the right-hand button of the mouse to 'listen' to text when using Clicker 4 grids).

Mousers

As quickly as possible, the school is equipping every room with the Mouser. Since using the Mouser in ICT lessons, the boy mentioned above has grown in confidence and enjoys greater independence. He still needs a watchful eye as his enthusiasm can cause him to make mistakes. For other lessons, he uses a laptop computer with Microsoft Word and Penfriend (a software application that sits alongside Word and offers predictions for the next word to be typed, thus speeding up word processing for switch users). The Mouser connects a joystick and small jelly-bean switch. He also uses a Compact keyboard with guard.

Encouraging independence

Independence is central to the whole of the curriculum and indeed pervades all aspects of school life. It is made clear to all staff that they have a responsibility to enable pupils to take control of their environment and gain independence. This is a global statement and applies to education in the whole. 'The ability to exercise control over one's environment is an essential prerequisite for the development of skills related to decision making and problem solving' (Banes and Coles 1994: 8).

For pupils with profound and multiple learning difficulties, they can learn that a switch operates a fan or a light and hence develop understanding of causes and effects. For those pupils with physical difficulties who do not have accompanying learning problems, a more complex control system may be of benefit in later life. A switch may be used to have the curtains drawn, turn on the radio/CD or unlock a front door to let in a visitor.

At Blackfriars School, every effort is made to overcome any passivity in pupils and staff work collaboratively to plan and deliver activities that are both accessible and self-motivating to the individual. These encourage progression for the pupil and confidence across a range of settings and with a variety of people.

Team working and professional development

One of the keys to the success of ICT at Blackfriars School is that of the ICT team (although all staff have ICT competencies). The core team consists of the ICT coordinator, a part-time ICT teacher, an ICT instructor (who works with the pupils in our Further Education Department) and an ICT support manager. For a special school, this is an unusually large and significant team that reflects the importance that is placed on ICT. The ICT coordinator has developed an enormous depth of understanding and expertise in the use of ICT to support learning and communication and to provide curriculum access.

This expertise is increasingly being recognized on a local and regional basis. The appointment, three years ago, of the ICT support manager has been absolutely crucial and much of what we are trying to achieve with the pupils would have been impossible without him. One of Her Majesty's Inspectors on a recent visit to look at the use of ICT in the school stated that his appointment had been crucial, both to the success of the new network and to the professional development of the other staff. In addition, the ICT support manager makes sure that all machines are functioning and sorts out day-to-day problems the staff face, which, if not dealt with promptly, can cause frustration and stress for the teacher. Particularly successful roles have been to develop the school's ICT website, advise other staff, extend the use of ICT to support management, provide on-line availability of the school's documentation and develop lunchtime computer clubs for the pupils.

The need to have staff with appropriate skills cannot be emphasized enough. Consequently, the continuing professional development of the whole staff in the application and provision of ICT is vital. Although the team, as outlined above, has been pivotal, they could not and should not be expected to take full responsibility for ICT development. It has to be a whole-school issue and be the responsibility of every member of staff. The successful use of ICT at Blackfriars School is dependent on the knowledge of every person who works with the pupil in the classroom environment: teacher, teaching assistant, volunteer, parent or pupil. In a recent monitoring exercise, staff members were asked to list all the benefits that they considered ICT gave the pupils. A comprehensive list was developed, the contents of which are summarized below.

The staff initially centred on the most basic function of the computer in relation to word processing and as a tool for presenting information, this being applicable to both pupils and staff. In relation to the latter, the ability to prepare well-presented teaching materials was identified, which is vital in particular for those with special needs. Specific to special needs pupils, ICT was seen to provide:

- Access to writing for pupils with poor fine and gross motor control and ease in storing and retrieving work, since the use of ICT aids fine motor control and hand–eye coordination.
- A means of drafting and redrafting that is easy, efficient and accessible and so is a great equalizer in presentation. This is particularly important for those pupils following externally accredited qualifications. Pupils are also enabled to create pictures, patterns and designs.
- Encouragement for children to work individually, independently and to be an active participant in the classroom, not just a passive observer. Pupils can work more quickly and demonstrate different types of writing exercise and have the opportunity to experiment.
- A way to enable pupils to get down in writing their own ideas and not those of adults working with them and thus demonstrate their true ability.

In addition to word processing, ICT was seen to be central to many special needs pupils who have little or no expressive language. It introduces ways of using augmentative and alternative communication approaches, facilitates social communication and interaction, and helps include pupils in the wider community. Peripherals such as switches, Powerlink and sensory equipment allow pupils with greater degrees of disability to have independence and choice. Information and communications technology enables pupils to use writing-with-symbols programs (such as Inclusive Writer) to support both reading and writing. As long as suitable software is available, all subjects within the curriculum can be supported. Finally, staff members believed that ICT introduces pupils to technology that they will need in everyday life, is highly motivating, helps concentration, has 'street-credibility' and is fun.

These illustrations show vividly the role and, indeed, *power* of ICT with individual pupils, in a class group and in a school as a whole. Power is an important word to use. Information and communications technology not only enables but also empowers many of the pupils in a way that would not be possible without access to this technology:

> The power of this continually developing technology, for pupils with special educational needs, lies in the way in which ICT can provide access to learning, whether that access be physical, cognitive or supportive. It enables them to take advantage of their entitlement to a broad and balanced curriculum.
>
> (Day 1995: 8)

Frustrations and difficulties

Naturally, there are negative aspects. In the above monitoring exercise, the following were seen as the key frustrations and difficulties:

* machines/software not working at the time you wish to use them;
* machines going down at the wrong moment and losing work;
* time and staff to ensure that machines are appropriately set up for every pupil at the time and in the place they require them;
* lack of staff to support pupils in the technology they are using;
* computers not updated regularly enough to run all the software required;
* time to look at and assess new software and to research software availability;
* lack of funding for software;
* lack of licences to give access to all software staff and pupils require.

What this list demonstrates is that many of the issues centre on funding. In the last eight years, Blackfriars School has spent in excess of £180,000 on ICT but this is insufficient. To fully provide everything that both staff and pupils require is currently beyond our means. It causes not only frustration but also means that we are not totally meeting the needs of all pupils. The failure to provide what is required and to give the staff the time to be able to make the maximum use of ICT is an area of concern with no ready answers – apart from greatly increased funding, which for the foreseeable future is not an option. It can cause high amounts of stress and, on occasions, has been noticed to make some staff negative towards ICT. The technical issues, although annoying, are the same as for anyone else working in the field of ICT.

Outreach

In 1997, Blackfriars School was named in the Annual Report of Her Majesty's Chief Inspector of Schools as one of the most effective special schools in the country. As a result of this, it was invited to apply for 'Beacon School' status and subsequently became one of the first 75 Beacon Schools in England and Wales. As ICT had been at the core of its curriculum for so long and as it had accrued a great deal of expertise in this area, it was decided that this should be one of its areas of outreach and sharing of skills with other schools.

Through the Beacon Initiative the school, among other outreach activities, was committed to:

* providing a support service for special needs children in mainstream

schools, particularly those having physical difficulties, and so help to maintain their inclusion in this sector;
- offering support to those special schools who feel they may benefit from the expertise of Blackfriars in the area of ICT;
- providing support for mainstream and special school staff in the use of ICT with special needs children.

The service that has been offered is:

- an ICT assessment for special needs pupils with a physical difficulty in any type of school;
- advice on the most appropriate hardware, peripherals and software;
- access to a resource bank for a limited loan period;
- pupil and staff support, for a fixed period of time, in the use of ICT;
- a telephone, fax, e-mail and website information service;
- in-service training.

This service is offered either at the school or in the mainstream/special school, whichever is the most appropriate, and is a completely free service.

The initiative took off beyond all expectations and has demonstrated the vital role that special schools have in supporting the mainstream sector. Between September 1998 and March 2002, the school provided training for 1500 teachers and learning support assistants from 230 different schools in the use of ICT to support special needs. During the planning phase of this project, it was anticipated that the numbers would be far fewer and that the majority seeking support would come from special schools. The number of requests surprised us, as did the fact that 96 per cent of those participating came from the mainstream sector.

When the initiative began, there was much apprehension in the school. What could we offer other schools and, in particular, what could we offer mainstream schools? This is an anxiety felt by many in special schools. They fail to recognize the vast wealth of expertise and knowledge that they contain. Personal experience has shown that mainstream schools are open to support and that there is an enormous need for the specialist help that special schools can provide. What appeared to be particularly attractive to mainstream schools was that the training was being provided by practising teachers, in the context of a school setting – and that it was free!

Theoretical aspects took place in the ICT suite at Blackfriars School and participants were then given the opportunity of seeing ICT in practice in the teaching and learning environment of the classroom. This practical aspect gave validity and credibility to the information being exchanged. It has also had a positive impact on the Blackfriars staff members involved, who have grown significantly in confidence and who now recognize the skills and expertise they possess, which bodes well for future outreach.

As these courses for colleagues in mainstream schools progressed, it became clear that there was a pressing need to provide professional development for learning support assistants. In many instances, without appropriate training (sometimes with no training at all), they were expected to work with identified special needs pupils. The amount of training provided was often limited. Their training needs and the vital role they play were often not recognized. Consequently, we designed courses specifically for them.

The response of learning support assistants to the training we have provided for them has been astounding. They have found the training extremely helpful and, more importantly, it has increased their motivation and morale. Through it, they have been recognized as key workers on whom the success of special needs pupils in the mainstream sector is so often dependent.

As a result of the courses the school has run, ICT staff members in school have been called into schools to offer individual or departmental support and, in several instances, to run training days for the whole school staff. In such instances, the course is tailor-made for the needs of that particular school and of its staff. The courses offered, which have been requested by mainstream colleagues, have included:

- *An introduction to Clicker 4*. This software is a cross-curriculum tool for writing and communication that has many features particularly suitable for children with special needs.
- *Technology to support access for all*. This is a broad-based course designed to illustrate how ICT can help children with special needs to be included in mainstream educational settings.
- *Ways to support recording*. Looking at supportive writing technology and software and how they can be used in classrooms.
- *The use of Microsoft Excel and Powerpoint as teaching tools to support special needs*. These standard packages can be adapted flexibly and imaginatively in supporting and teaching many children with special needs.
- *Software to support literacy and numeracy for pupils with special needs*. An introduction to different software packages and teaching strategies found useful in practice.
- *ICT for curriculum planning*. Packages such as IEP Writer (see Chapter 9) may be unfamiliar to mainstream teachers, who could find them helpful in developing an individual education plan for a statemented pupil.
- *The Internet and e-mail for special needs pupils*. Teachers in mainstream settings may underestimate the importance of teaching children access skills for the Internet and ways of using e-mail.
- *Making tables and templates with Word and Publisher*. Again, these standard packages can be used to great effect with special needs children to produce, for example, worksheets, rotas and timetables, perhaps with pictures of symbols for children with difficulties in reading.

Classroom management

For inclusion to be successful, and for special needs pupils in mainstream schools to be provided with the most appropriate opportunities, good classroom management is vital. From work with staff and pupils in mainstream schools, the following have been identified as good practice:

- determine whether a computer or other device is required to allow the pupil to engage effectively in learning;
- assess their access needs and provide peripherals and furniture appropriate for the individual;
- timetable the use of ICT to be an integral part of the curriculum;
- if only one computer is available, set short tasks so that all pupils have some access;
- identify the different levels of need and differentiate tasks;
- plan lessons so that those pupils with disabilities and learning difficulties can be fully included in the classroom;
- present meaningful, relevant tasks that are achievable using technology suitable to the individual;
- set a short-term target that the pupil understands;
- set tasks that are similar in nature to those in which the pupil's peers are engaged;
- avoid locating pupils with special needs at the edge of the group or class because of the location of the computer or the learning support assistant;
- provide opportunities to timid pupils and encourage independence and confidence;
- provide computer clubs at lunchtime or after school.

Looking to the future

So what of the future? The relentless development of ICT means that the school is constantly looking ahead to ways in which it can extend its skills and knowledge and provide even more effective support for special needs pupils in mainstream schools. Areas for development have been clearly identified in a recent and successful joint submission, with a local (mainstream) high school, to the Department for Education and Skills for Technology College status. There is a commitment that during the next five years, the areas listed below will be developed and implemented. Some refer to the improvement of ICT opportunities within the school. Other proposals are directed to supporting mainstream schools, the local community and businesses who have agreed to be 'partner businesses':

- To improve the availability of and standard of accreditation in ICT for all at Key Stage 4 and to raise standards at Key Stage 3.

- To develop consistent provision of videoconferencing for languages and international links. In particular, an international link with Namibia is to be established to foster in pupils a greater global awareness and understanding and provide a real audience and purpose for the development of ICT skills.
- To extend vocational and learning opportunities for Key Stage 5 pupils by establishing ICT links with local colleges for the purpose of distance-learning packages.
- To enhance the learning opportunities of the pupils in partner schools by making the ICT staff available one day a week for both technical and curriculum support, provide in-service training on the use of software and peripherals and to provide a telephone support line.
- To extend the skills and aspirations of identified gifted and talented Year 9 pupils in the partner schools by the development of a Saturday Club to foster ICT as a research, study and learning aid that can be applied across the curriculum to raise standards.
- To ensure that pupils in partner schools, absent due to physical or medical conditions, do not fall back academically and have the opportunity to continue their school studies by the production of an on-line homework resource provision.
- To extend free ICT courses to parents and families of pupils in the partner schools (both to develop their personal skills and to enable them to better support their children in the use of ICT) and to employees of business partners, as part of the school's work as a UK-Online Centre.
- To give support to the wider family of special needs children in partner schools and to involve them more closely in the learning process by providing a weekly updated information website, a database of parents with special needs pupils who do not mind being approached by parents in a similar situation, and a message board.
- To enhance the educational and social opportunities for people living in an urban regeneration area by the provision of a cyber café.

Conclusions

The outreach developments will extend the school's involvement in ICT into new realms that a few years ago would not have been thought possible. The implications are both exciting and challenging, as they will place significant demands on the school and the staff. But the pull and power of ICT means that they have to be pursued in the same way as the young teacher at the beginning of this chapter, nearly 30 years ago, had to pursue technology for the benefit of Doretta.

What the last 30 years of unbelievable advances in the microchip technologies and computer software have demonstrated is that, although technology in the right hands is a wonderful tool, it will never overcome physical disability completely – it is not a magic wand. In the words of the charity Ability:

> The technology available today to empower and enhance the lives of disabled people is extensive, varied, exciting stuff – but there are no magic wands here. Nothing removes the disability itself, and the real solutions take flexibility, patience and some effort . . . even after the right technology is chosen.
>
> (AbilityNet 1998: 4)

Products

- AbleNet Powerlink: Enabling Technology, 82 Oxhey Avenue, Oxhey, Watford WD19 4HA, UK.
- Alpha Smart: AlphaSmart Europe Ltd, Northway House, 1379 High Road, Whetstone, London N20 9LP, UK.
- Clicker, Ameba, Touch Games, Build, Switch On, Build + Reaction Timing: Inclusive Technology, 35 Charter Gate, Quarry Park Close, Moulton Park, Northampton NN3 6QB, UK.
- Mouser: Granada Learning Limited, Quay Street, Manchester M60 9EA, UK.
- SENSwitcher: dowloadable from: http://www.northerngrid.org/sen/intro.htm.
- Splatter: University of Manchester Institute of Science and Technology, Sackville Street, Manchester M60 1QD, UK.

References

AbilityNet (1998) *Computing for Life: Realising the Potential of Disabled People – With a Little Help from (Electronic) Friends*. Warwick: AbilityNet.
ACE Centre (2000) *Giving Control*. Unpublished document. Oldham: ACE Centre.
Banes, D. and Coles, C. (1994) *IT For All*. London: David Fulton.
Day, J. (1995) *Access Technology: Making the Right Choice*. Coventry: NCET.

7

USING VIRTUAL ENVIRONMENTS WITH PUPILS WITH LEARNING DIFFICULTIES

Penny Standen and David Brown

The potential of virtual environments in special education

Computer-based learning has enjoyed an increasing role in mainstream education with the development of more powerful personal computers available at a lower price. Computer-delivered instruction has also started to make a contribution to the education of children with learning difficulties. According to Hawkridge and Vincent (1992), it enables pupils to take charge of their own learning. Pupils with learning difficulties will find stimulation through 'enjoyable repetition' and a gradual increase in level of challenge: 'Words like "handicapped" and "disabled" imply dependence and powerlessness: with computers, learners can be less dependent and more capable' (Hawkridge and Vincent 1992: 25). More recently, Blamires (1999) has argued that enabling technology provides access for children to educational opportunities and life experiences, and facilitates engagement with knowledge and people: 'Speech, pictures, words, and animation can be combined in interactive ways to structure concepts to suit the level of understanding of learners and their interests' (p. 1).

Interactive software encourages active involvement in learning and gives the user the experience of control over the learning process. This is especially important for people with learning difficulties. Learners can work at their own pace. They can make as many mistakes as they like without irritating others and the computer will not tire of the learner attempting the same task over and over again, or get impatient because they are slow or engrossed in particular details. These benefits have been available since the earliest teaching machines and the first micro-computers. In recent years, however, the vast increases in computing power and memory have made it possible to introduce new levels of realism in software design – the virtual environment.

Virtual environments, for people with learning difficulties, have been described by Cromby *et al.* (1996) (see also Standen *et al.* 2001). Virtual environments (frequently known as 'virtual reality') are computer-generated, three-dimensional environments which respond in real time to the activity of their users. The most publicized examples involve wearing a head-mounted, stereoscopic display, headphones and various physical feedback devices that transmit and receive data. In these total-immersion virtual environments, information about the user's head and body movements are continually being fed back to the computer, which redraws the visual display in real time in response to the user's activity. However, virtual environments can also be experienced on a desktop system so that the environment is displayed on an ordinary computer monitor just like conventional computer games. The user moves through the apparent three-dimensional space shown on screen, and interacts with items in the environment using standard computer input devices such as a keyboard, mouse, joystick, spaceball or touch screen (Figure 7.1).

So, for example, in a virtual supermarket (see Figure 7.2), the user would be able to enter and move around between the aisles of goods with the aid of the joystick or the arrow keys on the keyboard. Items could be selected from the shelves by clicking on them with the mouse or touching them on the screen.

In addition to being more easily available, one of the advantages of desktop systems is that the public nature of the display permits inter-actions between the learner and a tutor or a peer. A tutor working beside the learner can create an atmosphere in which learning is enhanced through maintaining the learner's attention, through sharing activities and by assigning meaning to the learner's behaviour by relating it to material they already know or to concepts they are trying to grasp. The importance of working with a tutor in this way was highlighted by Vygotsky (1978), who used the term 'zone of proximal development' to refer to the gap between what a child is able to do alone and what he or she is able to do with the help of someone more knowledgeable or skilled than him- or herself. Although the ideal tutor is seen as being a sensitive and responsive adult, there is some evidence that learners also benefit from working alongside a peer (Topping 1992).

Cromby *et al.* (1996) draw attention to three characteristics of virtual

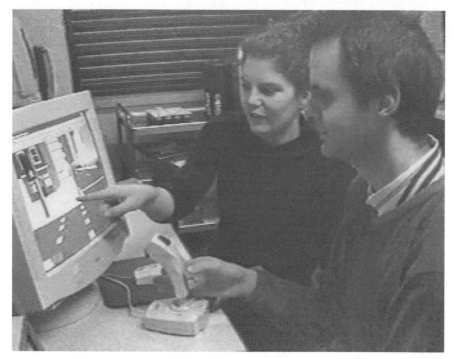

Figure 7.1   Using virtual environments.

environments in addition to those shared with other forms of computer-delivered education, which make them particularly appropriate for people with learning difficulties. First, virtual environments create the opportunity for people with learning difficulties to learn by making mistakes but without suffering the real, humiliating or dangerous consequences of their errors. People with learning difficulties are often denied real-world experiences that might promote their further development because their carers are apprehensive of the consequences of allowing them to do things on their own. Accompanied visits to a real environment sufficient to learn a skill may be impossible to arrange. However, in the virtual environment they can go where they like – even if their mobility is restricted.

Secondly, virtual worlds can be manipulated in ways the real world cannot be. In the real world, the learner can only be provided with 'scaffolding' (for example, human support or self-help manuals) because the world itself cannot be changed. As the learner becomes familiar with elements of the task, the scaffolding or training support is removed little by little. Finally, when the task is completely learned, all scaffolding will have been removed and the apprentice is doing the job without assistance. In a virtual environment, however, worlds can be constructed in any way the designer or teacher requires. A simple world could be constructed first,

Figure 7.2 Virtual supermarkets.

for example. Learning tasks are attempted in it. As the user becomes more familiar with the tasks, more complex worlds can be substituted. In fact, there are many ways in which the designer can manipulate the virtual world to provide graded assistance to learners.

Thirdly, in virtual environments, rules and abstract concepts can be conveyed without the use of language or other symbol systems. Virtual environments have their own 'natural semantics' (Bricken 1991), in that the qualities of objects can be discovered by interacting with them. For example, when crossing the road in a virtual environment, the learner does not have to grasp the conditional statement, 'If you cross when the light is red you may get hit by a car'. They can learn what happens if they cross at the wrong time by experiencing the virtual version of the consequences. Virtual environments can thus be used to facilitate concept attainment through practical activity.

Transfer of learning

Although virtual environments possess all these positive characteristics and are considered to be a safe arena in which to acquire and practise skills, it is essential that skills learnt in this way transfer to the real world where they are required. This has traditionally been a criticism of computer-based teaching, particularly for people with learning difficulties, but it does seem that virtual environments can show good generalization from skills acquired within them to the real world.

Initial work suggests that virtual environments are effective in facilitating the acquisition of living skills and that these skills can transfer from the virtual to the real environment. Standen *et al.* (1998) describe a study which involved taking 19 pupils aged 14–19 years with severe learning difficulties to a supermarket to find four items on the shelves and take them to the checkout. Nine pupils spent twice-weekly sessions carrying out a similar task in a virtual supermarket. The remaining pupils had the same number of sessions using other virtual environments. There was no difference between the two groups on their first visit to the real supermarket. Yet, on their return visit, those who had practised shopping in the virtual supermarket were significantly faster and more accurate than those who had not.

Another study by the same team assessed whether youngsters starting at a special school could be helped to become familiar with their school by exploring a virtual model of it. Twenty-two pupils aged 7–19 years, who were just starting at a special school, took part in this (unpublished) study. Pupils were again divided into two groups. The first group experienced the usual school-orientation course, which consisted of seven sessions learning to find 16 markers in the real school. The second group spent these sessions finding the markers in the virtual school. On the eighth session, a teacher who did not know to which group the participants belonged tested all the pupils in the real school in their attempt to find a random selection of the markers. There was no difference between the two groups in the total time spent with the tutor over the seven training sessions, so neither group had a differential advantage in the time they spent learning. The results of the study showed that the group who had learned on the computer had found significantly more markers by the end of the seventh session than had the group who had explored the school in reality. In the eighth session (the test session with a different teacher), there was no real difference between the two groups in the time taken to reach each marker. Nor was there any difference between them in the number and types of clues given once these figures were adjusted for the number of markers found. The fact that the computer group performed no worse than the other group is evidence that the learning they experienced in the virtual school transferred to the real one.

Both of these studies demonstrate transfer with virtual environments designed on a purely intuitive basis. Characteristics of the virtual environments that promote optimal transfer still need to be investigated. However, knowing that transfer takes place means that this issue moves down the list of priorities for researchers, who can turn their attention to other research questions.

The role of teachers

The introduction of new technologies has frequently led to predictions that they will revolutionize education. Unsurprisingly, often these claims are not realized. According to Light (1997), many new technologies have been offered to education as panaceas in the past, only to provoke the reaction that 'the only successful piece of educational technology is the school bus'. Talking about computer use in general, Hope and Odor (cited in Hawkridge and Vincent 1992) reported a growing suspicion that teachers would transfer old instructional techniques on to new media, and thus not fully exploit their potential. To avoid this happening with virtual environments, educators must take a proactive stance towards the growth of this important technology, rather than the reactive stance that has often been taken to educational technology developments in the past. 'If educators want virtual environments to meet learning needs, especially of those pupils who have unusual learning needs, they must play an active role in the development of applications, offering to developers their unique understanding of learning styles and good teaching practices' (Salem Darrow 1995: 2).

Rostron and Sewell (1984) see computers as just 'one more useful facility in the general remedial framework that is available' (p. 9), but advise that they are not there to replace human teachers, just to provide them with additional teaching aids. Although computers are highly motivating, Rutkowska and Crook (1987) caution against the naive belief that unguided interaction can effectively exploit their educational potential. There are two ways that interaction can be guided in this form of learning: through the involvement of a human tutor and through incorporating tutoring functions into the software.

The work described above using virtual environments was carried out with desktop systems, where the public nature of the display allows interactions between the learner and a tutor. However, in both schools and day centres, staff are responsible for too many pupils to be able to give one-to-one tuition on a regular basis and when they are able to provide this function they need guidance on effective strategies. According to Hawkridge and Vincent (1992) teachers need help and encouragement to build their confidence and skills in using computers and deserve proper training opportunities. At the time of writing, our research is concerned with discovering effective strategies in assisting pupils with learning difficulties to use virtual environments as a first step to provide the support that teachers need and to refine the software design to take over some of the roles of the tutor. So, for example, software developed by Wakung Chuang of Nottingham Trent University aims to help children with learning difficulties to acquire the skills of safely crossing the road. The virtual environment depicts several scenarios in which one might cross the road; for example, where there is no designated crossing place, at a pelican crossing and at a road junction. The density of traffic and the presence of parked cars can be varied to provide virtual environments that become increasingly difficult as the learner progresses. For each version of the software, two forms exist: one with a virtual tutor and one without. The virtual tutor provides information by visually highlighting the crossing route and by providing audible feedback (either verbal or non-verbal) when the learner achieves a goal or makes an error, for example by stepping into the road outside a designated crossing area.

Standen and Low (1996) shed some light on the teaching practices associated with the use of virtual environments in special education. Specifically, they looked at whether virtual environments did enable learners to take charge of their own learning or whether teachers were using them in a more conventionally didactic manner. Eighteen school-aged pupils with severe learning difficulties and their teachers were videotaped while using an educational virtual environment. Teachers' activity was coded into eight categories (e.g. instruction, suggestion, pointing) and the pupils' into three (e.g. whether he or she moved in three-dimensional space) and intra-rater reliability was established. Teacher activity significantly decreased as the sessions progressed. However, this decrease was not as marked as the increase in rates of pupil behaviour. This is because some behaviours (teachers' moves, physical guidance and instruction) fell at a faster rate, whereas others (suggestions) hardly changed. The interpretation of this could be that teachers are not just becoming fatigued but selectively dropping the more didactic and controlling behaviours. This can be explained with reference to the term 'scaffolding', identified by Wood *et al.* (1976) as one of the functions of teaching and described earlier in this chapter.

Another function of the teacher or tutor according to Wood *et al.* (1976) is to maintain the learner's interest and motivation by drawing their attention to relevant features of the task, by interpreting discrepancies between the child's productions and correct solutions and by controlling the frustration experienced by the learner. This was represented by the categories of pointing and suggestion, which decreased at a slower rate. These findings support the hopes expressed by some (e.g. Light 1997) that the teacher–pupil interaction that occurs with computer-based learning has the potential to reduce more didactic forms of teaching. An important research and development task is to determine whether some of these functions can be incorporated into the software, either in the form of unintrusive tutoring (giving advice but not preventing actions) or intelligent software tutoring (providing feedback based on the tutoring agent's experience of the task and the learner's behaviour). Such a software tutor would enable a less experienced person – even a peer – to carry out the function of maintaining the learner's interest and motivation. The benefits of peer tutoring are reviewed by Topping (1992).

To collect information to inform the design of software tutors and to provide advice for human tutors, Standen *et al.* (2002) examined what strategies human tutors used when working with adults who were learning to use virtual environments and how effective these strategies were. Data were collected on 20 people attending a social services day service for people with learning difficulties, described as having moderate to severe learning difficulties. They worked through four virtual environments: pelican crossing, café, supermarket and factory, all of which presented the learner with a series of tasks (e.g. ordering and paying for drinks in the café). Learners used the joystick to move around the environments and a standard two-button mouse to interact with them. Each participant spent a session using a two-dimensional routine to learn how to use the mouse. Once this had been mastered, they moved on to the other environments in the same order, only progressing to the next once a defined level of mastery had been achieved. Sessions were scheduled twice a week and lasted approximately 30 minutes. They were recorded on videotape, the camera positioned to view both the tutor and the learner sitting next to them.

The teachers' behaviour was coded into five categories:

- *Specific information* given to the learner about achieving a goal. It was further categorized as being about the mouse, the joystick or the environment (e.g. 'Go over to the bar now').
- *Non-specific information* did not provide the help that a learner needed to achieve a goal, but made the learner aware of possibilities and was similarly categorized as concerning the mouse (e.g. 'Where are you going to click then?'), the joystick or the environment.
- *Gesture* covered any movement made by the tutor, including pointing to direct attention to the screen, or to instruct movement of the arrow on the screen, or to direct movement through the environment.
- *Touching controls* included the tutor putting their hand over the learner's hand or taking over the input device to demonstrate. It was further categorized as involving the use of either the mouse or the joystick.
- *Feedback* could be either positive, such as praise or reassurance, or negative, which was rarely the case.

The behaviour of the learner was categorized in terms of the number of goals they achieved in an environment and could be either positive (finding an item on the shopping list) or negative (stepping into the road before the light has turned to green).

Although learners achieved approximately the same number of goals during each session, tutors' contributions to each session varied between earlier and later sessions. In the early sessions, tutors provided much more *specific* information, whether about input devices ('Use the mouse for that') or the environment ('You have to go through that door') than they did in later sessions. A similar pattern of change was shown in the frequency with which they used gestures. This suggests that, for the learner to achieve goals in early sessions, the tutor needs to provide more directive or controlling instructions. Levels of *non-specific* information remained high throughout all sessions, although this largely consisted of information about the virtual environment (e.g. 'What do you think is in there?'). So in spite of having to give more specific information in early sessions, tutors still found opportunities to maintain the learner's engagement and to put their activity into a broader context. Similarly, rates of both positive and negative feedback showed no significant change from the early to the later sessions. Negative feedback was almost non-existent, since all tutors used frequent praise and reassurance to maintain the learner's motivation.

The distinction between 'specific' and 'non-specific' information follows work on children's learning (Wood *et al.* 1976) that highlighted the different amounts of control a teacher might have over a pupil. The changes in teacher behaviour during the study described above suggest that this distinction is worth maintaining. The tutors appeared to be following the expected pattern of intervening or controlling less and less. In turn, this allowed more time for the teacher behaviours that maintain the learner's interest and motivation and which help to interpret the learner's activity. Giving less specific information did not cause the learner to make more errors, which supports the judgement of the teacher in reducing their prompts.

The distinction between levels of teacher control might also correspond to that which can be written into virtual reality software as distinct from those that need the presence of a human tutor. For example, specific information and feedback could be written into the software. Similarly, gesturing was largely used by teachers either to draw the learner's attention back to the screen or to draw their attention to a salient feature. The latter function could be incorporated into software by making a particular feature more prominent.

While such modifications could not provide all the functions of a human tutor, they would allow the human tutor to concentrate on other aspects of the tutor role. For example, the human tutor could valuably provide the non-specific information that maintains the learner's interest and motivation. They might also allow for the possibility of a peer acting as a tutor. In mainstream education, cooperative learning and peer tutoring have been investigated as a cost-effective deployment of teacher time. This might free the teacher from the stress of monitoring a large group and leave additional time for the more complex instruction that only a teacher or peer can provide. Topping (1992) reviewed a range of studies to show that peer interaction can support the learning of both specific and general skills. One advantage is that the learner might experience more practice through staying on the task for greater proportions of contact time. They might also enjoy the companionship, possibly responding on a personal level better to peers than to a teacher. Peer tutoring has had limited use in special needs education. With careful matching of the peer, the learner and the task, more could perhaps be done in this area in future.

The barrier of input devices

Many people with learning difficulties can find it difficult to control input devices skilfully. All our previous work with three-dimensional software has utilized a computer joystick for navigation tasks and a standard two-button mouse for interaction tasks. The reason for this choice was that earlier studies by members of our team had concluded that a joystick limited to two simultaneous degrees of freedom was easiest to use for navigating the virtual worlds. Alternative affordable and robust interaction and navigation devices were considered but the joystick was more suitable for *navigation* tasks than a keyboard or mouse. For *interaction* tasks, the touch screen and mouse were equally effective, although the touch screen used then was difficult to calibrate.

In a recent study, Lannen *et al.* (2002) describe their work with a standard joystick and mouse performed to identify the specific difficulties experienced by young people with learning difficulties. Each pupil was asked to complete navigation and interaction tasks, using the joystick and mouse respectively, within a virtual factory, café or supermarket. Demonstrations of the devices and tasks were given before commencing the evaluations. Measures taken included:

- misuse of the device (non-task-related movement, harshness, pressing the wrong buttons, etc.);
- support required (spoken instruction, physical assistance, etc.);
- physical difficulties (insufficient strength, inability to grip properly, etc.);
- user comments and reactions.

Some of the difficulties users experienced were due to physical ability (or the interaction of this with the device construction). For example, when using the joystick they frequently gave *too* much left/right deflection, repeatedly pressed the button even though it produced no effect on the software, had to have the base held still by the examiner or experienced difficulties gripping the mouse. Other difficulties appeared to be related to the user's cognitive understanding of how to use the devices; for example, occurrence of random movement and frequent pressing of mouse buttons. Finally, difficulties arose as a result of the design of the virtual environments, which led to several pupils requiring physical help to complete some tasks. For example, one pupil required physical assistance with the joystick to align his position in front of the exit doors in the virtual factory, since the area that triggered the door opening was too narrowly defined.

In the study by Standen *et al.* (2002), much of the time spent by the tutor in the learner's early sessions was on providing assistance with the input devices. Less time was given to help with the mouse than with the joystick (in fact, the first teaching session had included specific training on using the mouse). Users experienced problems in remembering what tasks were accomplished by each device and in moving from one device to the other as many used the same (dominant) hand for both devices. These findings have led to another of our current studies, which is to design a new input device or devices to make the control of virtual environments easier for users with learning difficulties. Otherwise, the difficulties our users experience with the devices can too often be frustrating and demotivating. As a first step in designing a new device, 40 users of a day service have helped us to document the difficulties they find with current devices and to evaluate the first prototype (Standen *et al.* 2003). One or two input devices corresponding to the tasks of navigation and interaction may be needed, but it may also be the case that the same design may not suit everyone and that different versions of the product will need to be produced.

Conclusions

The research and development work that we have described in this chapter, on the use of virtual environments as an educational aid for people with learning difficulties, suggests that they have potential in helping with the acquisition of skills, which would increase independence and wider community access. Although the development of such technology still has far to go, our work does suggest ways in which educators could make more use of virtual environments in the classroom. First, it is very much the case that teachers are needed to support pupil work in virtual reality. Virtual reality, like any computer aid, is not there to replace human tutors. Rather, it offers an additional teaching opportunity.

Secondly, while the original idea behind virtual environments was to allow the pupil free exploration, many children benefit from being given specific goals to achieve. Our virtual factory was popular because pupils enjoyed finding (in one exercise) the complete set of health and safety forms, which stacked up like the scores in a game. This does not preclude allowing pupils to roam around the virtual environment and explore it, but this usually happens when they have gained some familiarity with the environment. Familiarity is more easily obtained while engaged in some form of goal-directed activity. One young man with severe learning difficulties and autism enjoyed moving around on the ceiling of the virtual supermarket and it took the first author some time to realize that this was a deliberate choice rather than an error he could not correct.

Thirdly, our work on tutors' strategies suggests that, while the tutor must initially provide a great deal of assistance and advice, the pupil can eventually continue to achieve goals in the virtual environment without this help as long as the tutor provides positive feedback. As with all successful learning, the secret probably lies in presenting tasks that are initially easy and later of increasing complexity. Some software currently in development recognizes this and allows the tutor to provide increasingly challenging environments. So, for example, an environment to teach crossing the road varies the traffic density and the number of parked cars at the roadside.

A prime consideration throughout has been to keep costs down and make the system user-friendly so that this aid to learning is widely available and usable by as many people with learning difficulties as possible. Our potential customers are schools, day and resource centres and voluntary organizations, who have limited funds. Although we have links with commercial distributors, there is little prospect of selling enough copies to keep the price within potential purchasers' budgets. Some of the software is already available as freeware via a variety of project websites. One such example is software to develop work-based skills in horticulture, ICT, catering and self-determinism for people with low skills. This is available for download at www.flexiblelearningsystems.net. Other software can be obtained by contacting the second author.

Development has been slow to cater for users with visual impairments, although acoustic virtual environments are being developed elsewhere. While interactive multimedia may not appeal to everyone it does, in the words of Rostron and Sewell (1984), provide 'one more useful facility in the general remedial framework that is available' (p. 9).

Acknowledgements

The authors wish to acknowledge the ESRC (award number R000223018) and the EPSRC (award number R21851) for their support with research cited in this chapter and Steven Battersby for Figure 7.2.

References

Blamires, M. (ed.) (1999) *Enabling Technology for Inclusion*. London: Paul Chapman.

Bricken, W. (1991) Training in virtual reality, in *Proceedings of the 1st International Conference on Virtual Reality*. London: Meckler International.

Cromby, J.J., Standen, P.J. and Brown, D.J. (1996) The potentials of virtual environments in the education and training of people with learning disabilities, *Journal of Intellectual Disability Research*, 40: 489–501.

Hawkridge, D. and Vincent, T. (1992) *Learning Difficulties and Computers*. London: Jessica Kingsley.

Lannen, T., Brown, D.J. and Powell, H. (2002) Control of virtual environments for young people with learning difficulties, *Disability and Rehabilitation*, 24(11–12): 578–86.

Light, P. (1997) Annotation: computers for learning – psychological perspectives, *Journal of Child Psychology and Psychiatry*, 38: 497–504.

Rostron, A. and Sewell, D. (1984) *Microtechnology and Special Education*. London: Croom Helm.

Rutkowska, J.C. and Crook, C. (1987) *Computers, Cognition and Development*. Chichester: Wiley.

Salem Darrow, M. (1995) Increasing research and development of virtual reality in education and special education: what about mental retardation? *VR in the Schools*, 1(3): 1–7.

Standen, P.J. and Low, H.L. (1996) Do virtual environments promote self-directed activity? A study of pupils with severe learning difficulties learning Makaton sign language, in P.M. Sharkey (ed.) *Proceedings of the First European Conference on Disability, Virtual Reality and Associated Technologies*, Maidenhead (http://www.cyber.rdg.ac.uk/ISRG/icdvrat).

Standen, P.J., Cromby, J.J. and Brown, D.J. (1998) Playing for real, *Mental Health Care*, 1: 412–15.

Standen, P.J., Brown, D.J. and Cromby, J.J. (2001) The effective use of virtual environments in the education and rehabilitation of pupils with intellectual disabilities, *British Journal of Educational Technology*, 32(3): 289–301.

Standen, P.J., Brown, D.J., Horan, M. and Proctor, T. (2002) How tutors assist adults with learning disabilities to use virtual environments, *Disability and Rehabilitation*, 24(11–12): 570–7.

Standen, P.J., Brown, D.J., Anderton, N. and Battersby, S. (2003) The development of control devices for virtual environments for use by people with intellectual disabilities, in *Proceedings of the 10th International Conference on Human–Computer Interaction*. Mahwah, NJ: Lawrence Erlbaum Associates.

Topping, K. (1992) Co-operative learning and peer tutoring: an overview, *The Psychologist*, 5: 151–61.

Vygotsky, L.S. (1978) *Mind in Society: The Development of Higher Psychological Processes*. Cambridge, MA: Harvard University Press.

Wood, D.J., Bruner, J.S. and Ross, G. (1976) The role of tutoring in problem solving, *Journal of Child Psychiatry and Psychology*, 17: 89–100.

8

MANAGING SPECIAL EDUCATIONAL NEEDS PROVISION WITH ICT: INDIVIDUAL EDUCATION PLANS AND BEYOND

Allison Rees and Anna Williams

The management of special educational needs (SEN) provision is a key part of meeting the needs of individual and groups of pupils and raising levels of achievement for all. This chapter considers how SEN provision is managed in mainstream schools by reviewing the role and responsibilities of the special educational needs coordinator (SENCO) and considering which aspects of the coordinator's role can be developed through the use of information and communications technology (ICT). We argue that ICT offers an opportunity to plan effectively, manage SEN provision and practice and, in so doing, help raise achievement for pupils with SEN.

The role of the special educational needs coordinator

Before 1994, staff in schools could devise their own systems for managing and monitoring SEN provision. However, this changed with the introduction of the *Code of Practice on the Identification and Assessment of Special Educational Needs* (Department for Education 1994). The *Code* stated that all mainstream schools should have a 'designated teacher' whose responsibilities included:

- the day-to-day operation of the school's SEN policy;
- liaising with and advising fellow teachers;
- coordinating provision for children with special educational needs;
- maintaining the school's SEN register and overseeing the records on all pupils with special educational needs;
- contributing to the in-service training of staff.

Since the introduction of the *Code*, these designated teachers, known as special educational needs coordinators, have become key members of staff within schools. Some coordinators are part of the senior management team within a school, though their positions vary. In very large schools, the coordinator may be full-time with a SEN teaching commitment; in smaller schools, a teacher may be released part-time or the head or deputy may take on the responsibility of the coordinator. However organized, all schools have a designated member of staff who fulfils the role of the coordinator. In 2001, the role was strengthened by a new *Special Educational Needs Code of Practice* (Department for Education and Skills 2001a), which replaced the 1994 *Code*. The new *Code* states:

> The SEN Coordinator (SENCO), in collaboration with the head teacher and governing body, plays a key role in determining the strategic development of the SEN policy and provision in the school in order to raise the achievement of children with SEN. The SENCO, with the support of the head teacher and colleagues, seeks to develop effective ways of overcoming barriers to learning and sustaining effective teaching through the analysis and assessment of children's needs, by monitoring the quality of teaching and standards of pupils' achievements, and by setting targets for improvement
> (Department for Education and Skills 2001a: §5:30–1, p. 50)

Clearly, making provision for pupils with SEN takes place at several levels. Within a class context, this encompasses the planning and development of appropriate learning opportunities for individuals and for groups of pupils. Making provision may include identifying resources and, in some cases, allocating and training additional staff. At a whole-school level, it includes managing staff, developing systems to assess and monitor progress, disseminating information and working with outside agencies. Enabling teachers to identify SEN, address 'potential barriers' to learning and support pupils are challenging tasks coordinated by the special educational needs coordinator.

Managing SEN with ICT

The revised *Code of Practice* (Department for Education and Skills 2001a) states that headteachers and governors should support the special educational needs coordinator in the use of ICT for SEN management systems and for preparing and recording individual education plans (IEPs). However, there is little literature about the use of ICT in the management of SEN. But as Hewer (1992) predicted, pupil records are increasingly likely to be held on electronic databases. Special educational needs coordinators may or may not have the requisite skills to use electronic databases, as they 'are usually chosen for their ability to work with pupils with SEN, not for their prowess at using a computer' (Stansfield 1996: 24). Our experience in mainstream schools suggests that there is some, but not universal, uptake of ICT to write IEPs and keep records, despite an increasing number of software packages designed for this purpose.

Mumtaz (2000) suggests that the factors limiting the use of ICT in schools include lack of experience, lack of availability of a computer and poor on-site support. Robertson *et al.* (1996) supported this view and also noted time management and lack of support from the school administration as additional reasons for limited use. Phillips *et al.* (1999) suggest that limited access to ICT may be a factor explaining why primary schools have lagged behind secondary schools in the development of computerized record-keeping and administrative systems, as there are relatively smaller numbers of pupils with SEN in each individual school.

However, in a recent review of IEPs, Gross (2000) noted that 'more and more schools are now accessing computerised systems with banks of targets and related strategies, which allow large numbers of IEPs to be produced at the click of a mouse' (p. 126). Gross is sceptical about this increased use of ICT to generate IEP targets and achieve progress. She argues:

> The targets may have been made up by the SENCO sitting at home with her paperwork or they may have been spawned by a computer programme. Even if the child was originally involved in agreeing targets, the chances are that no one has reminded him or her of them since then.
>
> (Gross 2000: 128)

If Gross is correct that the use of ICT in making and managing provision for pupils with SEN is increasing, then her comments serve as a pertinent reminder that *how* schools use software programs is important. As Constable (2002) reminds us, the needs of the child must take precedence. We cannot necessarily expect the child to fit the software. For example, one of our reception class pupils has cerebral palsy and is not yet toilet-trained. The software package we use offers two targets – 'to ask for help to use the toilet' and 'to use the toilet independently' – but these are not sufficiently broken down to meet the learning objectives for this pupil. His IEP targets are 'to tell the teacher/support assistant when his pad needs changing' and 'to gradually increase the amount of time when the pad is removed'. However, the strategies suggested by the software – picture prompts, to try to establish a set time for the use of the toilet, praise – have been incorporated in the IEP. Here the software is regarded as a starting point for suggested resources and strategies used to help achieve the targets. The software offers general suggestions but the teachers insert the specific resources they intend to use.

To promote the use of ICT in the management of SEN, colleagues need to be convinced of the merits, usefulness and efficiency of any software program. There are two key areas within the role of the special educational needs coordinator that could draw on ICT programmes: writing plans for individual or groups of pupils and the management and maintenance of records. As suggested in the above example, this would include developing and recording appropriate IEP targets and strategies for achieving those targets. It could also include monitoring pupil achievements. In terms of the administrative duties, a quicker, more effective monitoring system than that which is currently available in the school would need to be included in the package.

Writing plans for pupils with SEN

The *Code of Practice* sets an expectation that pupils with SEN have an IEP. This remains a core part of the special educational needs coordinator's planning and monitoring role. The *SEN Toolkit* states:

> IEPs [individual education plans] should focus on up to three or four key individual targets and should include information about:
> • the short term targets set for or by the pupil
> • the teaching strategies to be used
> • the provision to be put in place
> • when the plan is to be reviewed
> • success and/or exit criteria
> • outcomes (to be recorded when IEP is reviewed).
> (Department for Education and Skills 2001b: §5, p. 2)

An IEP needs to be produced in a format that incorporates all this information. Additionally, the *SEN Toolkit* specifies that targets should be 'SMART', that is Specific, Measurably Achievable, Relevant and Time bound. Babbage *et al.* (1999: 36) note that 'an individual education plan (IEP) should outline in specific terms the next stage for a pupil and how that will be taught. The IEP should reflect the actual learning needs of the pupil in terms of objectives'.

The vision of the IEP as central to meeting the needs of pupils clearly identifies it as a fundamental area of work for the special educational needs coordinator and, in turn, a key area for considering how ICT can be used to support their development.

Managing and maintaining records

Under the earlier 1994 *Code*, schools were required to keep a SEN register, or list of pupils with SEN. This is no longer required, but most schools continue to keep 'lists' to record which pupils have SEN, as well as the level and form of provision required to meet pupil needs. This administrative role is often the most time-consuming aspect of the special educational needs coordinator's job. Reeves (1999: 3) describes it as 'considerable' and suggests that coordinators need to develop systems that are familiar to colleagues, and have a good balance between formal and informal procedures that are not too bureaucratic. He reminds coordinators that 'A great deal of your time is likely to be taken up by administrative procedures but it is always important to keep things in perspective and remember that the purpose of these procedures is to enable children to learn and make progress'. Such procedures need to record and track progress if the system is to promote learning rather than be a summative record of achievement. If ICT is to play a key part in the management of SEN provision, programs which support the special educational needs coordinator in writing IEPs and in the administration of provision are welcome supports.

Though there are several software programs designed to support the development of IEPs, we provide an in-depth look at one (IEP Writer) and consider how this program has enabled SENCOs to develop their own practice, manage IEPs and monitor provision of SEN in one outer London local education authority. This is not an endorsement of a particular program, as all commercially available programs have many features in common and school staff will have many considerations to take into account when selecting a program for a particular school.

IEP Writer

IEP Writer (1998) was developed by special needs teachers from nursery, primary and secondary schools with the assistance of speech and language therapists and special schoolteachers. It is designed to be used in mainstream and special schools and it enables teachers to create an IEP quickly and easily.

IEP Writer identifies targets in book form or on CD-ROM. There are five databases available – Literacy, Numeracy, Behaviour, Communication Skills and Early Level Targets. Each database is divided into sub-sections.

The IEP Writer Early Level Database is compatible with the P-scales (Department for Education and Employment 1998) and covers literacy, maths and personal, social and health education (PSHE). The targets are broken down into very small steps to allow all pupils to achieve success. The Early Level of reading identifies targets in foundation reading skills, book skills, early reading skills and phonic skills. The Early Level Database would also be appropriate for pupils who are still working on the 'stepping stones' in the Foundation Stage Curriculum (Department for Education and Employment 2000). For example, the targets for a pupil working on rhythm and rhyme, and therefore at the yellow/green 'stepping stones', could be 'to respond to rhythm' or 'to recognize and complete rhymes'. These would link directly to identified areas of the communication, language and literacy sections in the Foundation Stage Profile, which will be used to assess all children approaching the end of their reception year, which is also at the end of the Foundation Stage.

The IEP Writer Literacy Database includes targets in reading, writing and spelling extending from the pre-skills to higher-order skills. The list does not claim to be complete and targets can be adapted to reflect the levels of attainment for individual pupils. An IEP for a pupil with dyslexia may include a target such as 'to read and spell regular words with initial consonant blends'. However, the teacher would need to make this target more specific by identifying the blends to be taught and learned. The pupil may require a particular structured approach to learning the blends and this must be incorporated in the target. Commonly pupils will confuse letters with similar shapes and patterns, for example b/d/p. The suggested target would read 'to recognize b and d'. The achievement criteria clarify this further by adding, 'able to distinguish the two letters on some teacher specified number of separate consecutive occasions'.

The IEP Writer Maths Database is a comprehensive list of targets covering all aspects of numeracy, shape and space, and measurement, including time and data handling. The basic skills in this database are based on organization and concentration and reflect ways of working rather than basic mathematical concepts. This then moves on to number recognition and counting; targets in this section could be linked to the Foundation Curriculum and used for pupils in early Key Stage 1. The more complex targets for division, for example 'knowing that division is the inverse of multiplication', would be appropriate in Key Stage 2 and beyond.

The IEP Writer Behaviour Database identifies behaviour in a range of settings, reflecting the different expectations in contexts. The 'Behaviour in the Dining Hall' is a particularly good example of SMART targets that could be monitored by midday assistants. The targets are practical and unambiguous. Assistants are encouraged to have reward strategies, which can target and promote positive behaviours. The targets include examination techniques appropriate for older pupils.

Speech and language therapists and teachers devised the IEP Writer Communication Skills Database. It includes targets for expressive and receptive language, auditory memory, vocabulary development and verbal reasoning. Although the database is comprehensive, it is essential that class teachers understand the developmental needs of their pupils and this may mean that the targets are set collaboratively with a speech and language therapist. Indeed, the database reference sheets remind teachers that they should seek the advice of a speech and language therapist. For example, a teacher may select a range of targets linked to phonemic awareness to promote this aspect of literacy within a class of pupils. This may be age-appropriate for the class but inappropriate or impossible for a child with articulation difficulties. A pupil with oral dyspraxia may have developed auditory discrimination but be unable to pronounce individual phonemes. Teachers need to recognize the order of sound production as well as developmental stages and the specific difficulties experienced by some pupils.

IEP Writer 2 (2001) offers an update of the original program, including:

- compatibility with the 2001 *Code of Practice*;
- an increased number of targets;
- an increased capacity to include more information on an individual education plan (for example, for noting strengths/areas of difficulty);
- secure password protection;
- a capacity to import/export pupil details from other administrative systems (for example, SIMS).

Case example: using IEP Writer to produce IEPs

The *Special Educational Needs Code of Practice* (2001a) suggests an IEP should contain three or four targets. IEP Writer allows the teacher to select a maximum of five targets. Limiting the number of targets focuses the teacher's thinking and encourages priority be given to the greatest areas of need. This avoids a wide spread of targets across several skills, which the pupil would be unlikely to achieve within a realistic timescale.

The danger is that using software to produce IEPs can become a 'button-pushing' exercise as teachers faced with deadlines may make decisions and judgements based on a cursory review of the database, rather than individual pupil formative assessment data. Our experience has shown that teachers are amazed at the ease at which an IEP can be generated. Entering the data and asking the computer to generate a plan has a 'wow' factor. However, writing IEPs must *not* become a button-pushing exercise. It is important to understand the nature of the pupil's difficulties and recognize individual priorities for teaching and learning.

It is important that expectations are not solely based on the target list; gaining a broader perspective on the pupil's abilities will need to be considered. Identifying the current level of attainment does not inform the teacher of *how* the pupil has been able to work towards that achievement, or indicate the learning processes involved. Teachers must use their professional judgement in determining levels of attainment for each pupil.

Entering the data and identifying targets

In our experience, the use of IEP Writer varies from school to school. In some schools, the class teacher, in discussion with the support assistants, enters the data and a completed IEP is given to the special educational needs coordinator. Or the coordinator may be given a list of target statements for each child and enter the data. Although these strategies have as much to do with the ICT skills of the individual teachers and familiarity with individual education plan databases, they are time-consuming, though they provide a perspective on the overall SEN within the school. A key drawback to software systems such as IEP Writer is that teachers can become very focused on setting the targets and there is little or no discussion with the pupils.

In ideal circumstances, the teacher is given release time and the special educational needs coordinator is available to work alongside them to discuss the pupil's strengths and area of difficulty, select targets and identify key priorities. Working through the list of targets and exploring the sequence of progression may lead to greater insight into the pupil's learning strategies. Though some may argue that such a strategy is unrealistic, we would argue that this is time well spent. It is essential that there is 'ownership' of the IEP by both teachers and pupils and that the final plan is a personal working document. Otherwise, IEPs may be filed away and not looked again until the review.

Producing the IEP

The format of the IEP is determined by the choice of presentation from the program in both portrait (Figure 8.1) and landscape (Figure 8.2) versions. You can set your own layout and this is useful because it is possible to combine or delete columns and produce a working document for your school. The columns are clear and it is possible for all staff to quickly gain

Individual Education Plan

Name	Sam Worker	**Stage**	School Action
Area/s of concern	Literacy, Maths	**Year group/IEP No.**	Y3
Class Teacher	Mrs Calm	**Start date**	May 2003
Supported by	Mrs Cool	**Review Date**	July 2003
Proposed Support		**Support began**	January 2000

Targets to be achieved	**Achieved**
To multiply a number by 10 / 100 / 1000.	1.
To combine multiples of coins to make £1.	2.
To read Orange Level of reading scheme.	3.
To answer comprehension questions based on a story / play / poem.	4.

Achievement criteria
Responds correctly to written / verbal questions on three separate occasions.
Accurate when tested on three occasions and applied in practical contexts / classwork.
Reads with minimal support and is able to answer questions about the books.
Accurate when tested on three separate occasions.

Possible resources and techniques
Verbal questions. Textbooks / worksheets. Base 10 blocks. Abacus. Numbers arranged as patterns.
Real / plastic coins. Computer 'shopping' programs. Classroom 'shop'.
Reading-scheme books and appropriate worksheets. Flashcards and games to reinforce sight-vocabulary.
Verbal questions. Comprehension activities and worksheets based on the story.

Possible strategies to use in class
Ensure that Sam has understood the concept of place value. Link multiplication by 10/100 to work with
    money.
Set practical activities for finding as many ways as possible of combining coins to make £1.
Listen to Sam read at least once a week. Maintain home-school reading record.
Ask relevant questions about the books Sam is reading. Set comprehension activities.

Ideas for support teacher / assistant
Encourage Sam to look at patterns of numbers and observe that the digits move one place to the left when
    multiplied by 10.
Allocate time for 'shopping games' to teach equivalent combinations of coins.
Listen to Sam read at each session. Discuss the story. Provide activities to reinforce sight-vocabulary.
Discuss books with Sam. Set comprehension activities.

Parents / carers need to
Listen to Sam read. Write in the reading record book. Make sure books are returned to school each day.

Student needs to
Read as often as possible. Remember to bring books back to school.

Copy for parent / teacher / support / file

Figure 8.1   Portrait individual education plan.

information and identify the approaches to be used in planning and working with the pupil. IEP Writer has the potential to produce many IEPs and contain a vast amount of data. This can be used in a summative way to reflect the profile of special educational needs within a school.

Individual Education Plan

Name	Mary Tryer	
Area/s of concern	Literacy	
Class Teacher	Mr Black	
Supported by	Ms Helpful (Senco), Mrs Angel (LSA)	

Start date	May 2003
Proposed Support	in-class support daily, small group withdrawal 2 x 15 mins per week

Stage	SA
Year group/IEP No.	Y2
Review Date	July 2003
Support began	April 2002

Targets to be achieved	Achievement Criteria	Possible resources and techniques	Possible strategies for use in class	Ideas for support teacher / assistant	Outcome
To write two sentences under a picture with the support of a wordbank.	Three pieces of work completed.	Any picture with wordbank provided. Words to use for writing displayed on classroom walls.	Provide picture to write about or use Mary's own drawing. Supply list of spellings.	Talk about the picture and support the writing of sentences.	
To use capital letters for the personal pronoun 'I' and for the start of sentences.	Accurate on three separate consecutive occasions.	English textbooks and worksheets. Computer programs.	Demonstrate the use of capital letters. Encourage Mary to think about using capital letters in her writing.	Provide exercises for Mary to punctuate.	
To leave even spaces between words.	Achieved on three separate consecutive occasions.	Squared paper. Use the space bar on a computer. Exercises to put spaces in appropriate places.	Remind Mary before she writes that spaces need to be left between words.	Watch as Mary writes and remind that spaces have to be left. Provide activities to reinforce spacing.	
To position writing on the lines.	Accurate on three separate consecutive occasions.	Dots to follow. Tracing over letters. Copying. Hand control exercises. Guidelines.	Correct as appropriate. Provide handwriting activities.	Give opportunity to trace and copy letters. Provide paper with guidelines.	

Parents / carers need to

Student needs to Try to write two sentences independently. Take care when writing.

Figure 8.2 Landscape individual education plan.

Extending the IEP

In addition to enabling teachers to identify targets, IEP Writer links the statements with achievement criteria, possible resources, strategies and ideas for support staff. Each target has suggestions for parents, carers and pupils to complete, support and consolidate learning.

There has been some debate about whether an IEP needs a separate section outlining achievement criteria, as it could be argued that 'SMART' targets include achievement criteria. However, measurable achievement criteria may act as a guide for monitoring progress. Often support staff seek clarification on the frequency that a pupil has to achieve a target for it to be 'learnt'. Therefore, achievement criteria that can be measured by frequency or duration can be helpful.

Possible resources include a range of general resources. Which resources are available to support individual pupils should be discussed with the special educational needs coordinator to ensure that the pupil has opportunities to use a wide variety of appropriate materials. Finding new and exciting resources is a constant 'challenge'. Teachers may require support in identifying materials kept in school, particularly new materials and the ways in which they may be used. For example, the use of practical equipment to support the maths targets can be a useful reminder, particularly with older pupils who continue to need 'concrete' experiences to understand concepts.

Strategies include a range of ideas with overarching aims. For example, strategies linked to targets on addition include: 'Set exercises to practise adding by counting on. Provide a number line or other apparatus for support'. Further advice for the support teacher is given as 'Provide practical activities to reinforce adding by counting on e.g. items on a shopping list'. The strategies rely on some degree of professional knowledge and, in some instances, might require explanation if they were given to less experienced staff, for example 'ask inferential questions based on a picture or text', 'talk about implicit information within the text'. However, IEP Writer also includes ideas for support assistants. These sections may be helpful in directing the staff to develop work tasks. Although some of the statements are general, for example 'Provide sequencing activities', they are useful for initiating a discussion about what resources are available. They also encourage those involved with the pupil to discuss strategies and *how* materials are used.

Finally, the sections specifying what parents, carers and pupils need to do may produce conflicting views. On the one hand, they may be a supportive reminder to the parent/carer/pupil to complete tasks at home. Alternatively, they can make the parents feel guilty, adding to their worries. Although government advice says that all pupils should be given some homework, some parents feel 'challenged' by this expectation and the content of some of the tasks. The advice given in the final individual education plan tends to be practical and reflect the type of 'homework' routinely given to pupils, for example practising spellings or hearing your child read. However, the presence of the suggestions does not guarantee that the work takes place!

IEP Writer in action: learning from experience – a case study

Our experience of the introduction of IEP Writer produced mixed reactions. The majority of staff welcomed it, but it was not without teething problems. One of the initial problems was the availability of the program. With a five-user site licence, it was difficult to decide which were the best machines to install it on. We did not get this right at first and some members of staff did not have the program available on a PC near to them. The program is now installed on the network but limited to five users, although it is rare that five users require it at once.

A further problem was the lack of time to write IEPs in school. Previously, staff members were able to write IEPs at home but they could not do that with this system. A limited amount of release time is now given to staff to meet with the special educational needs coordinator to draw up plans. Staff consult the database printouts and prepare their ideas, resources and strategies in advance so that a plan can be drawn up quite quickly. An up-to-date list of SEN resources is useful to have available so that appropriate resources can be entered on the IEP.

After using IEP Writer for two years, we feel it has enhanced the quality of the IEPs that we produce. For example, an IEP written before the introduction of IEP Writer, may have given a target as 'improve word building'. Under the *Code of Practice* this target is not SMART, as it is not specific and measurable. Using IEP Writer, the class teacher would be prompted to clearly identify areas within this target to be developed. The target using IEP Writer could read 'to read/spell CVC words with vowel sounds "a" and "e" ' or 'to be able to segment words with 2/3 syllables for reading and spelling'. Although the development of SMART targets does not require software, our experience is that it has been particularly valuable and supportive for newly qualified and less experienced staff or for pupils with more complex needs, where it is sometimes difficult to identify the key focus of the IEP.

Our technician adapted the templates to the format of the local education authority so the IEPs are professional-looking, contain relevant targets, strategies and resources and are valuable working documents. As one newly qualified teacher recently said after writing her first IEP using IEP Writer, 'Is that it? I thought it would take me hours!'

Does IEP Writer produce meaningful IEPs?

In terms of writing IEPs, IEP Writer offers special educational needs coordinators and teachers a useful package. *How* the program is introduced to staff and used to produce IEPs requires careful planning and monitoring. IEP Writer enables teachers to produce plans that have clear targets focused on the specific needs of the pupil. All targets, resources and strategies can be easily adapted for individual pupils. The suggestions for strategies and resources enable a teacher to plan effectively to achieve the targets and thus promote learning.

Using the criteria defined by the *SEN Toolkit Section 5* (Department for Education and Skills 2001b), the IEPs written using IEP Writer are SMART, show targets, strategies, provision including resources and identify success criteria. The range of databases enables staff to consider the steps towards supporting pupils 'overcome their barriers to learning' as defined in the National Curriculum (Department for Education and Employment 1999). Although IEP Writer databases support staff in decision making about targets, they are not without their critics. Mittler (2000) warns that the focus on behavioural objectives and SMART targets may narrow learning opportunities, particularly as many commercial IEP schemes tend to be defect-orientated. It is as important to remember what pupils can do when setting targets. The use of software packages such as IEP Writer should *support* the process of developing a plan. It does not supplant professional knowledge and expertise.

It is essential that the procedure to draw up the IEP involve all parties if it is to be meaningful and lead to effective learning. The inclusion of suggestions for parents and pupils highlights potential work to be practised in the final plan, but staff in schools must ensure that parents, carers and pupils are involved earlier in the process. Their views should be *actively* sought. The *Special Educational Needs Code of Practice* (Department for Education and Skills 2001a) includes a chapter on 'parent partnership' and identifies the key role of parents/carers in their child's education. The *Code of Practice* also states:

> Children and young people with special educational need have a unique knowledge of their own needs and circumstances and their own views about what sort of help they would like to help them make the most of their education. They should, where possible, participate in all the decision-making processes that occur in education including *the setting of learning targets and contributing to IEPs* [individual education plans].
> (Department for Education and Skills 2001a: §3.2, p. 27; emphasis added)

It would be easy for staff to become focused on target setting to the exclusion of the pupil, particularly if they work to pre-determined lists at home or on the computer. In heeding Mittler's (2000) warning, it is an important responsibility of the class and subject teacher to include pupils in decision making about their IEPs. The child's view of a 'priority' may differ from those of the staff. In addition, reviewing targets and providing an opportunity to celebrate success can be motivating and raise self-esteem.

However, writing IEPs is only one of the roles of the special educational needs coordinator. The coordinator managerial role encompasses maintaining records, collating information and managing provision. To effectively 'manage' SEN provision, the coordinator needs to be able to list pupils with SEN, with information about their level of need, by school and class. They need to be able to track progress by monitoring targets and coordinate the overall provision by reviewing the success of strategies and areas of support. As a program for producing IEPs, IEP Writer is limited as a data management tool, although the newer version, IEP Writer 2, can be used in conjunction with other administrative systems, thereby broadening its potential.

The company that produces IEP Writer offers a compatible administration system called Special Needs Register+ (SNR+). This system enables the special educational needs coordinator to compile a database of all pupils with special educational needs and allows access to information on individual pupils, class or year group as well as whole-school summaries. Using SNR+ would complement IEP Writer 2 and address the management issues. Information from the company's website suggests it is possible to:

- Input pupils' details and automatically list by class, year group, gender, Special Educational Needs (SEN) level, area of concern
- Access a summary list of all pupils on the register, their levels and year groups
- Add additional information about each pupil (could include Ethnic Code, Date of Birth, a database code, test results, agencies involved and so on)
- Produce custom letter printouts in conjunction with Microsoft Word
                    (http//www.iepwriter.co.uk/other_products.htm)

When used in conjunction with IEP Writer™, SNR+ can do all of the above and has the following additional capabilities:

- to automatically produce the register of all children with individual education plans;
- to show current targets and achievement criteria;
- to produce review sheets showing targets and achievement criteria;
- to print a reminder of the reviews needed each month;
- to produce a monitoring and evaluation sheet.

The SNR+ enables the special educational needs coordinator to monitor pupils by area of need – learning difficulty, emotional and behavioural difficulties, physical, hearing or visual impairments. In practice, schools need to buy both IEP Writer *and* SNR+ to fully address the writing of IEPs *and* the management of SEN.

When evaluated against Stansfield's (1996) criteria for selecting software programs (see Table 8.1), IEP Writer/IEP Writer 2 perform well. Our experience has shown them to be time-saving and effective tools if used with forethought, as detailed in the following example.

Table 8.1   Criteria for selecting an ICT/SEN package (adapted from Stansfield 1996)

• Software that is easy to run on a familiar machine
• Programs save time and not make more work than a traditional process
• IT use should not take up time which might have been spent with pupils
• The package should not 'crash' or lose data
• It should be user friendly
• It should have a password to protect data and maintain confidentiality
• It should be adaptable to a school's needs

Good practice

IEP Writer is used widely across the local education authority, but where it is used most effectively the special educational needs coordinator 'manages' its use but class teachers write and own the IEPs plans for their class. Teachers discuss IEPs with the coordinator. The coordinator supports the teacher by giving advice and keeping him or her informed about additional information, such as assessment data and strategies provided by outside agencies, which may be relevant to the development of an appropriate IEP. The coordinator will have knowledge of the resources available to meet that child's SEN.

Each year, there is the opportunity for teaching staff to get to know their classes early in the autumn term before the IEP is written at the end of September. Teachers can then review the progress of pupils previously at *School Action* or *School Action Plus* and consider whether they are appropriately placed on the *Code*, have no further need of support or require specialist 'outside' advice. To accomplish this, the special educational needs coordinator sets clear deadlines for each step in the plan development process and the class teacher discusses issues with the coordinator as they relate to their own classroom planning and practice. This might include discussions about learning styles, possible strategies or differentiation. The coordinator gives INSET to remind/train staff in the use of IEP Writer with follow-up individual sessions where necessary. The class teacher then writes the IEP. The coordinator monitors the progress by reviewing a sample of IEPs from each class. Reviews are held twice a year. During the period the coordinator monitors progress, particularly for pupils at *School Action Plus*, support assistants are encouraged to keep notes that are added to the review comments. The IEP is used to inform practice and work targeted to meet the pupils' SEN.

Where software programs such as IEP Writer have been less effective is in schools with a high turnover of staff. Staff turnover means that fewer staff are able to use IEP Writer without support and the time required to train new staff might not be available. Moreover, while staff may be involved in discussions to set targets, the level of expertise varies. In such situations, the special educational needs coordinator must take a leadership role in developing IEPs while working to establish a system in which class teachers can take responsibility for writing their own plans. The coordinator might argue that in writing IEPs for the teachers, he or she has a better overview of the SEN in the school and that the targets are more SMART, but this has to be balanced with the need for teachers to become involved in writing meaningful plans.

Using SEN management software in YOUR school

In summary, our experience of IEP Writer has shown that software programs can be used to good effect in developing IEPs and potentially in the management of SEN provision, particularly if it is combined with other software programs. Stansfield (2002) supports the use of ICT in the administration of special educational needs, including the possible use of support assistants to undertake the 'clerical' part of the workload. Table 8.1 outlines her 1996 criteria for selecting an ICT/SEN package. However, in evaluating software programs against these criteria, it is important to remember that they do not replace the important role of formative assessment, teacher judgement or expertise, and care must be taken when introducing a commercial software program within a school or local education authority.

It is also important to remember that the involvement of the child at every stage of the development of the IEP is essential and the plan needs to be monitored and evaluated. As users of IEP Writer, we would encourage special educational needs coordinators to consider the use of software programs such as this, bearing in mind the concerns that have been raised about some aspects of their use. We suggest the following guidelines:

- It is essential to have a focused introduction to the program, including a demonstration and opportunity for all staff to 'play' with the program.
- Although the list of targets is extensive, it is necessary to 'personalize' them for individual pupils.

- To gain a full picture of a pupil's level of attainment and learning preferences, support assistants, parents, carers and pupils should be included in discussions.
- It is essential that the school identifies its own resources and offers support to the staff in the use of materials.
- Software programs may have to be configured to fit local education authority requirements. As IEPs are generated only two or three times a year, staff benefit from 'step-by-step' guides that can prompt them with key questions they need to ask when selecting targets.
- To fully develop, monitor and manage provision for pupils with SEN, the school may need additional compatible software programs (for example, to list pupils and generate class and school records).

Conclusions

The use of ICT can enhance the role of the SEN coordinator in the management and provision for SEN. IEP Writer is an example of a program that supports staff in writing IEPs for pupils and groups and enables them to consider a range of targets, strategies and success criteria. The use of an additional program for administration and management of the 'lists' of pupil need and level are desirable. However, factors that will influence the initial commitment to the use of ICT and the effective implementation of programs to support SEN work are likely to be determined by staff confidence and management issues within the school. Any new initiative needs to be negotiated with staff, a clear policy has to be drawn up for its use, and access to equipment and adequate training must be provided. DeLyon Friel notes:

> Technology adds a twist to the jobs of educators and necessitates some important problem solving. The solutions to the problems, however, must evolve through the collaborative efforts of stakeholders. Thoughtful discussion and reflection are required, and differing viewpoints and philosophies must be addressed. The solutions must reflect the educational goals and expectations of each school and school system
>
> (DeLyon Friel 2001: 135–6)

Our experience of the introduction of a software program for developing IEPs was positive, though not without initial implementation difficulties. Recognition that there may be 'teething' problems, anxiety and reluctance on the part of some staff underscores the need to work collaboratively in introducing, managing and monitoring such programs. However, as noted at the beginning of this chapter, ICT offers an opportunity to plan effectively, manage SEN provision and practice, and in so doing help raise the achievement of pupils with SEN.

Products

- IEP Developer (computer software): Special IT Solutions Limited, Po Box 374, Cheltenham GL53 7YU, UK.
- IEP Manager (computer software): SMEREC, Granada Learning Limited, Quay Street, Manchester M60 9EA, UK.
- IEP Writer (computer software): Learn How Publications, 10 Townsend Avenue, London N4 7HJ, UK.
- IEP Writer 2 (computer software): Learn How Publications, 10 Townsend Avenue, London N4 7HJ, UK.

References

Babbage, R., Byers, R. and Redding, H. (1999) *Approaches to Teaching and Learning*. London: David Fulton.

Constable, D. (2002) *Planning and Organising the SENCO Year: Time-saving Strategies for Effective Practice*. London: David Fulton.

Department for Education (1994) *Code of Practice on the Identification and Assessment of Special Educational Needs*. London: HMSO.

Department for Education and Employment (1998) *Supporting the Target Setting Process – Guidance for Effective Target Setting for Pupils with Special Educational Needs*. London: DfEE.

Department for Education and Employment (1999) *The National Curriculum Handbook for Primary Teachers in England*. London: DfEE/QCA.

Department for Education and Employment (2000) *Curriculum Guidance for Foundation Stage*. London: DfEE/QCA.

Department for Education and Skills (2001a) *Special Educational Needs Code of Practice*. London: DfES.

Department for Education and Skills (2001b) *The SEN Toolkit Section 5: Managing Individual Education Plans*. London: DfES.

DeLyon Friel, L. (2001) Using technology appropriately: policy, leadership and ethics, in J.F. LeBaron and C. Collier (eds) *Successful Technology Infusion in Schools*. San Francisco, CA: Jossey-Bass.

Gross, J. (2000) Paper promises? Making the Code work for you, *Support for Learning*, 15(3): 126–33.

Hewer, S. (1992) *Making the Most of IT Skill*. London: CilT.

Mittler, P. (2000) *Working Towards Inclusive Education Social Contexts*. London: David Fulton.

Mumtaz, S. (2000) Factors affecting teachers' use of information and communicative technology: a review of the literature, *Journal of Information Technology for Teacher Education*, 9(3): 319–41.

Phillips, S., Goodwin, J. and Heron, R. (1999) *Management Skills for SEN Coordinators in the Primary School*. London: Falmer Press.

Reeves, G. (1999) The role of an SEN coordinator. *The SEN Coordinator's File 1.* London: pfp publishing.

Robertson, S.I., Calder, J., Fung, P. *et al.* (1996) Pupils, teachers and palmtop computers, *Journal of Computer Assisted Learning*, 12: 194–204.

Stansfield, J. (1996) Lightening the load, *Special Children*, January, pp. 22–5.

Stansfield, J. (2002) The ICT guide showing support, *Special!*, Autumn, pp. 52–3.

9

MANAGING INNOVATIONS IN ICT: ISSUES FOR STAFF DEVELOPMENT

John Hegarty

Helping staff to develop skills in using information and communications technology (ICT) is, in practice, a difficult thing to do. It is equally difficult for teachers to feel that they have a key part to play in developing the scope and quality of the ICT provision in their school. Schools and colleges, like any organization, have management structures and teachers have a variety of managerial roles and duties. A key one of these is the ICT coordinator, who is frequently looked up to as the fount of all wisdom and the repository of all knowledge in this area. This chapter reflects upon some of the skills and approaches that they require to be effective in supporting the development of ICT as a teaching tool for meeting the needs of all learners. It also considers the high levels of managerial skill in ICT that all teachers need if they are to use information and communications technology appropriately; indeed, successful ICT use requires a special mixture of professionalism both in the technical expertise and in the teaching aspects of ICT. This chapter identifies some of the key skills for teachers and ICT professionals with responsibility for meeting special educational needs.

ICT capability

In their challenging book, Kennewell *et al.* (2000) write about the concept of 'ICT capability': ' "Information and communications technology" refers to the set of tools used to process and communicate information; to be "ICT capable" is to be competent in controlling the situations in which those tools are applied' (p. 1). They go on to examine this idea in detail. They aim to help staff in schools to develop their use of ICT, which, as they point out, has a unique position in schools, in being a subject in its own right, a Key Skill, and a set of tools for learning. As has been shown in this book, it is also a set of management tools and a sophisticated set of personal resources that children and teachers use in many different ways in their personal and professional lives. Kennewell *et al.* believe that, if schools aim for greater ICT capability, the achievements of pupils in ICT, in and out of school, will increase. The specific components of this increased capability can be identified at the level of pupils, teachers, classrooms and management, and they argue for targeted staff and resource development programmes to develop ICT capability.

Web-supported learning: the Internet

The most pervasive and educationally far-reaching innovation in ICT is undoubtedly the Internet. The revolutionary nature of this for the teacher is apparent if we think of the time, not so many years ago, when stand-alone computers were the norm in schools and colleges. While some, better-equipped organizations had the luxury of having their computers linked in a network, the educational vision was limited to the software applications that were bought and installed. Who could have foreseen, then, the tremendous increases in the multimedia capability of personal computers now, and the opportunity to link with other computers throughout the world that the Internet has made possible. There are more and more opportunities to acquire software and resources from the Internet. This includes both sites that are specifically designed for teachers and those maintained by companies or organizations that have useful resources for special educational needs work. Examples include:

- National Grid for Learning (2002a);
- British Educational Communications and Technology Agency (Becta 2002a);
- Department for Education and Skills (2002a); and
- Widgit Software Ltd. (2002a).

There are also sites maintained by local authorities (e.g. Lewisham Borough Council 2002) that offer a selection of links to useful resources to teachers.

Far-thinking organizations, anticipating the growth in the use of Web-supported learning, are striving to make their websites more accessible to people with special needs. COMPASS, an online collection of 5000 objects from the collections of the British Museum, is one example, described in detail by Howitt and Mattes (2002).

Undoubtedly this trend in Web-supported learning will increase, so that we will see more and more classrooms with Internet access, and more and more computers in the classrooms connected. What are the implications of developing ICT capability for teachers of children with special needs?

A good illustration comes from a case study by a language teacher (Dimitriadi 2001) about teaching two children with dyslexia. Instead of relying on software specifically designed to help children with dyslexia, she introduced a multimedia authoring package, Hyperstudio, to the children and helped them to create a fantasy multimedia package. Basing the project on their interests, the pupils produced a presentation on 'Dinosaurs doing sports'. The children learned new skills, were motivated and creative. They acquired new vocabulary and their spelling skill improved.

Dimitriadi's project was innovative in the way technology (the multimedia capability of a personal computer) and a software application (a multimedia presentation authoring package) was used, rather than in those innovations themselves. Her article provides in fascinating detail how an imaginative teacher can combine knowledge of the children, an ideological stance of wishing to produce a child-centred project, technical knowledge about the software, and a desire to document and record the progress that children made. Another example of helping children to create multimedia presentations is given by Atherton (2002) in a companion volume in this series, *ICT in the Primary School* (Loveless and Dore 2002).

Multimedia innovations

Digital still cameras

Many teachers are finding digital cameras to be quite revolutionary for working with a range of pupils, especially those who have difficulty working with text and printed materials. Pictures can be straightforwardly printed out, used within photo-editing software, published on websites or e-mailed to friends and relatives. Cameras which store pictures on a removable floppy disc or cartridge have been especially welcomed by some teachers because they are so simple for pupils to use. In a project preparing people to move into more independent housing supported by The Home Farm Trust Ltd, cameras were in frequent use to help people plan not only what they wanted in their new homes, but who they wished to live with. The combination of ease of use, the ability to see the photograph instantly and the many possibilities for editing and displaying the pictures make these cameras one of the most essential pieces of educational technology in recent years. For example, it was good to see a young woman with Down Syndrome avidly photographing the Christmas cake-making activities of her class for later insertion into portfolios of work that would be submitted for external award schemes, such as the Award Scheme Development and Accreditation Network (ASDAN 2002). Indeed, the use of this technology is an example of the way in which, more and more, computers are not only useful in themselves, but are essential for other equipment to be used.

Combining media

What does one do with the images when photographed, besides putting them on a website or printing them out? They can be edited, using commercial picture-editing software. Or they can be combined into multimedia presentations. While there are specialist software packages to do this, the industry-standard Microsoft Powerpoint is a relatively easy way to compile presentations of pictures, sounds and text. An example is a presentation made in-house by a teacher at a school for pupils with severe learning difficulties, which combined video clips, still digital photos and simple text on health issues. It was designed for children to work through themselves. Another example comes from a college lecturer who produced an effective presentation for a pupil with (hitherto) short attention span and limited ICT, with his collaboration, which he could work through as an *aide-mémoire* for learning the steps of a work skill he needed to master.

Video projectors

In class, video projectors allow images normally available only on-screen to be seen enlarged, giving not only a much greater impact, but the added benefit that a group of pupils can see the picture at the same time. Video films can be shown and computer output of all kinds. What would normally be seen as a small image by one or two people can now be seen enlarged, and vividly (and with hi-fi sound with the appropriate equipment), by a large group at the same time. I was privileged to sit in on a 'computer' lesson with a group of teenagers with severe learning disabilities. The teacher explained that she had always found it difficult to use the computer with the whole group of ten pupils at once, and so had requested a video projector. Finally, the college authorities had approved the expenditure and she had used it for the first time the week before my visit. She said that it had revolutionized her lessons. As I watched, in the darkened room, the class members sat entranced as the teacher led them through the quizzes and animations of some software on basic mathematics. The frequent questions in the software were read out to the whole group and there were lively offerings of the right answers. Doubtless these projectors were originally intended for business presentations. Yet their use in schools has introduced valuable flexibility, diversity and visual appeal.

Digital video photography

The range of uses will be similar to that of still photography, but with the added dimension that video brings. Of course, videotape recorders have had widespread use in schools for many years, but there are new possibilities for computer-based editing with digital formats. With recordable CDs now available cheaply for computers, and digital videodisc (DVD) format increasingly widespread, 'home movies' of various kinds will bring subjects to life for many children.

Undoubtedly, a key area to exploit is in involving children with special needs in producing their own CDs incorporating still and video sequences. The British Educational Communications and Technology Agency has recently introduced its 'Creativity in Digital Video' awards to encourage teachers and children (in all areas of education) to do more with these media (Becta 2002c). A book providing examples of the use of these media is that of Fawkes *et al.* (1999), which gives a series of papers, scenarios and classroom case studies on the use of television and video with pupils with special educational needs.

Multimedia profiling

A special example of using multimedia is 'multimedia profiling'. This is an innovative way of combining a range of media (stills, video, sound, graphics and text) that has been developed by the charity Acting Up to help people with communication difficulties to express and represent themselves. An individual client is helped to compile a series of images that represent their daily life and activities. It is then stored on computer as a database of images. The individual can then browse these images of their life, or, with support, they can be compiled into a report. The approach allows people to express themselves, for example at review meetings, in a vivid and meaningful way. More information is available on the Acting Up website http://www.acting-up.org.uk/ (Acting Up 2002).

Videoconferencing

Help in introducing videoconferencing can be found in Arnold and colleagues' (2000) resource book for teachers on videoconferencing in the classroom. The book is free, comprehensive and beautifully produced. It portrays a range of possible uses for videoconferencing, with specific examples from the schools that took part in the project. These included schools sharing storytelling, toys they liked, village history and shared games used as 'ice-breakers'. The most valuable use for one special school was in accessing the help of a consultant to provide advice on specialized equipment for a pupil with profound and multiple learning disabilities (Mountjoy Special School, personal communication). A valuable website giving support, a list of schools using videoconferencing and lots of other useful information is given by the Arbour Vale School (Global-Leap 2002) in Slough.

The importance of support and evaluation

The need for support has always been recognized by UK governmental initiatives in ICT. The British Educational Communications and Technology Agency (Becta), like its predecessor organization, the National Council for Educational Technology, has an important role for teachers using technologies. Much of its early work was to do with the dissemination of information about the available technology and software, and ways in which it could be used for different groups of learners (including those with special needs). More recently, it has begun to address the need for the scientific evaluation of technologies and has managed a range of projects, some of which were very large, for example ImpaCT2 (Becta 2002b).

ImpaCT2 involved 60 schools in England (a representative sample of all schools) and it included some schools for children with special educational needs (although the main emphasis of the research was on the likely effect of ICT on examination attainment in primary and secondary school pupils). An important finding of the ImpaCT2 study was the widespread use of ICT across all school-age children, but with those using ICT at home having more frequent and more confident use. Primary school children spent three times longer on ICT at home than at school and secondary school pupils spent four times longer (Becta 2002b). Many children described the level of ICT use in school as infrequent and their access to the Internet as rare. In contrast, home use was frequent with considerable freedom. A similar picture of ICT usage at home and school is also presented in a report for the Department for Education and Skills (2002b). This extensive study showed that 99 per cent of children used computers at home, at school or elsewhere and, therefore, that computer usage was almost universal.

The reasons for this widespread use of computers at home include the lower cost of computers, the increasing penetration of the Internet into society and the general attractiveness of ICT to children. They use their computers for 'fun' things, be it game-playing, chat rooms and e-mail, accessing hobby sites, or working with music and pictures. In contrast, they tend to have less available time for ICT use while at school, where free access to the Internet is limited and where they will be constrained to work on syllabus-related topics. Thus, school ICT use is for 'work' and home ICT use is for 'pleasure'.

The picture in special schools and for children with special needs is less clear. While the ImpaCT2 study included five special schools (for children with emotional and behavioural difficulties, mild, severe and profound learning disabilities, and deafness), and also looked at the support of children with learning difficulties and with high attainments in mainstream schools, the diversity of children's needs made it difficult to paint a simple picture. In contrast to the detailed information the study gained from children in mainstream schools, there is little available information on the use of ICT by children with special educational needs (SEN) in special schools.

The implications are that children's ICT awareness and confidence will grow as much, if not more, through the influence of school as through their experience at home. This will pose a challenge for teachers to be aware of what children are able to do at home in the realm of ICT and what support they are able to have from parents and relatives. Work at home will not only reinforce that done at school, but may also be quite different. Sales of computer software that in the past might only be bought by schools are now being made available to parents, and educational software suppliers (such as Granada Learning/SEMERC) are targeting sales and information to parents as well as children (http://www.granada-learning. com/home/about/semerc.jhtml).

Internet use in special schools

The ImpaCT project carried out case studies of ICT use in two special schools, one for children who were profoundly deaf and hard of hearing, and one for children with emotional and behavioural difficulties. A different pattern of ICT use emerged. In contrast to what was happening in most mainstream schools, these children made extensive use of the Internet *in school* and networked technologies were found to be beneficial. Chat rooms, for example, facilitated communication in a safe environment and enabled pupils to control how they presented themselves. The Internet was valuable for research, permitting ready access to up-to-date and relevant information. Children used revision sites and search-engines to find information. For leisure, children used e-mail, chat rooms, downloaded music and played games (including multi-player on-line games). These applications were facilitated in school, in sharp contrast to the picture painted for mainstream children in mainstream schools. We still know little about their use at home, from this study, so further research is needed. Home use will depend upon the availability of computers there and the amount of parental encouragement. Nevertheless, a clear role for teachers to develop home use to support children's ICT skills is suggested.

In the ImpaCT2 study, the two schools for children with learning difficulties had only recently had Internet access. Abbott and Cribb's (2001) survey of Internet use in special schools confirmed that the rapid increase in Internet use in mainstream schools had not been mirrored in special schools. However, some special schools have been able to give a much higher priority to networked technologies, and their work is heralding what will happen in more and more schools as facilities and expertise increase. Exciting and innovative work in such schools is showcased in Abbott (2002).

Although it would appear that Internet use is taking off more slowly in special schools than in mainstream schools, projects such as those described above are looking to the interconnectivity of modern computers to offer a major and fundamental resource to the whole school: not simply to provide supportive curriculum resources, but also to celebrate the work of the school and the children in a unique way. Add to this the possibility of helping children form links with others across the world, and one is seeing tremendous innovation.

It should be noted that it is not just professionals who are making use of technology to showcase the special nature of the work they do. Individuals with disabilities also are using ICT to give a public face to their identity and to make contact with others. This is shown in unusual and interesting research by Jane Seale of Southampton University (Seale 2001). She systematically trawled the Internet to find examples of websites produced by individuals with special needs, or by families on the behalf of a learning-disabled member. Twenty personal home pages were found. Thematic analysis of their content, form and language revealed different ways in which page owners expressed and perceived their self-identity.

Effective ICT use

A moment or two's thought about what makes some classroom practices more educationally effective than others suggests where to look for a better understanding of effectiveness in the use of ICT in schools. A valuable insight comes from a little-known study by Goldman *et al.* (1987). They contrasted the hyperbole surrounding the educational effectiveness of microcomputers with the shortage of information to guide policy making. Their four-year study in the USA looked at the number of microcomputers in schools, how funding was organized and decisions were taken, and staff training. The researchers were interested in the organizational level and the administrative context of microtechnology. They argued that managerial practices are essential in determining whether the technology is in use and that such practices should focus on how much technology is actually used as well as auditing the use of microtechnology in special-school classrooms.

In the study of Goldman *et al.*, those evaluating the use made of microcomputers by schools were physically distant from the use of the technology. The report of it does not say exactly what the administrators ultimately did with the findings – were they simply filed or did they inform future practice? Were they fed back to the teachers? Ideally, teachers and their managers would regularly engage in systematic appraisal of how ICT is being used, and the findings of such audit would be used in a considered fashion to improve the effectiveness of classroom practices.

Action research to improve service quality

In the late 1980s, Jane Seale and I set about devising a way for teachers to carry out their own audits of ICT use in a way that would help them use ICT better. We were inspired by the pioneering work of Professor Jack Tizard on the quality of residential care for children and adults with learning disabilities (Tizard 1964). Following Tizard's model of evaluation and action research, Seale carried out a detailed study of how microcomputers were used with clients visiting an occupational therapy centre (Seale 1988). She visited the centre over several months and collected data in various ways: she observed what happened there during her visits; she interviewed the centre manager, the direct-care staff and occupational therapy aides; and she examined the records that were kept. The aim of gathering these data was to find a way to measure effective microcomputer use objectively. It was possible to identify features characterizing the centre's use of computers. These features included: the aims of microcomputer use for clients; frequency of use; the degree of staff interest in the microcomputer; access to and use of outside experts; and relationships within the organizational hierarchy (Seale 1988). The results were discussed in terms of the organizational context of innovation, which studies in the literature had identified as key aspects of innovation; in particular, its context, its locus, the degree of support available, mode of implementation and the available resources. Seale's overall conclusion emphasized the organizational context of innovation as much as the individual behaviour of managers: 'What emerges from this study is that we cannot look at individual managerial practices in microcomputer use in isolation from the organisation in which managers work, the people within that organisation, and the resources and expertise that are made available' (Seale 1988: 98).

In this study, Seale identified what structural sociologists might have thought unquestionable, namely that the organizational (social) structures within which individual staff members operate create pressures (such as role expectations) that determine individual behaviours. The main implication of the study is that microcomputer use, at the level of how effectively it is used with a client, is affected by organizational factors that are outside the control of individual staff members. This is an important conclusion, for it puts the onus for the effective implementation of new technology on the organization. It does not detract from the individual skill levels, teaching strategies or interpersonal interaction of staff with clients, but emphasizes that these factors alone are insufficient to guarantee effective use of new technology. The challenge for the organization is to ensure that their managerial strategies for implementing innovations in new technology are sufficient to ensure appropriately effective use.

In later studies, Seale (1993, 1998) undertook a detailed analysis of day centres for people with learning disabilities that were using microtechnology. The findings refined her 1988 study and suggested that managers of day centres needed to pay attention to five main aspects of computer use: resources, support for staff (both ideological and technical), involvement of staff, planning and the details of how computers are used. In her latest discussion (Seale 1998), she introduces the concept of a 'centre-focused' implementation strategy for microcomputer use. Drawing on earlier ideas of the need for a school-focused strategy of innovation, a centre-focused strategy 'places emphasis on the context in which the microcomputer as an innovation is placed [and engages] the whole centre or parts of it in a collective effort . . . a centre's culture, its behaviours, attitudes, beliefs and structures, create an environment in which a microcomputer has to survive' (p. 33).

As noted at the beginning of this chapter, helping staff to develop skills in using information and communications technology is difficult, yet it is vital that teachers feel that they have a key part to play in developing the scope and quality of the ICT provision in their school. Staff need the confidence that comes from having the necessary skills to support children's use of the technology and from the belief that they are truly supported by management. Teachers need to feel that the level of service it is offering, as a team, to children and parents is of the highest possible quality. The whole school needs to feel that they have the most up-to-date ICT equipment that is possible within budgets, and frameworks for using them that match curriculum and children's needs. This requires that staff in schools are able to make the element of their service explicit, get feedback on its components with appropriate audit, and put in place activities to develop the service further. To do this, they need audit tools.

Audit tools

Seale's research produced a questionnaire (for the Assessment and Management of Microcomputers in Adult Special Education, AMMASE) that could be used by an organization (or a unit within an organization, such as a class or department) to gather data on how it used ICT in certain key ways. It provided a profile of the managerial health of ICT use in terms of the resources, support, client involvement, planning and computer use that existed. The underlying idea was that if the organization gained the maximum score on each of these areas, then ICT use was as effective as it could possibly be.

Since Seale's work was published, it has been possible for many users of ICT with people who have special needs (including teachers, college lecturers and day service instructors) to apply the concepts underlying AMMASE to their own situation and many investigations have been undertaken as part of the coursework for the Diploma in Information Technology for Special Needs course at Keele University. These studies have included systematic audits of the ICT provision that have considered resources, ideological and practical support, and a range of parameters of use. In several cases, there have been significant pieces of work that otherwise would not have been produced, and they have stimulated detailed thinking about the quality of provision. Further details are available in Hegarty *et al.* (2000).

AMMASE is one approach to use, but others are available. A UK government survey of ICT in schools (Stevenson 1997) carried out a nation wide audit of ICT use in schools. The overall findings make interesting reading, but the list of 'key issues' provides useful headings for teachers to use to appraise their own ICT use. Hardy (2000) has some useful exercises for teachers to carry out with helpful forms to record outcomes. Chapter 6, in particular, discusses auditing staff use of ICT. Such published guides are helpful, but they may not be specific enough for auditing specific features of a school's, or a teacher's, use of ICT. In such cases, quality-audit principles come into their own.

Auditing ICT using quality standards

Quality-audit methodology offers a potentially valuable approach for everyday audit of ICT effectiveness. The principle of this approach is to begin by defining an objective quality standard. Note that 'quality' does not, in this sense, necessarily imply a high technological standard. The reasoning here is that 'quality' can never be defined absolutely, but requires qualification in terms of fitness-for-purpose. An inexpensive program of software designed to encourage children with profound and multiple learning difficulties to look at the computer screen and which meets this objective reliably is, in this sense, meeting its quality target. An alternative product, which, perhaps, is deemed to be of higher 'quality' in terms of its graphics and documentation, but which does not achieve the same objective, is actually not achieving its quality target.

The following is the approach used at Keele University as a starting point for teachers applying quality-standard methodology to an element of the service they are offering:

• Use documentation, or interviews with colleagues, to obtain clear statements of relevant general aims for the target of the audit.
• From these, write highly specific and measurable objectives.

- Now agree with colleagues the minimum level of achievement of each objective that would constitute a satisfactory standard.
- Implement a monitoring exercise to gather data on how far the objective is being met.

The reason for doing this could be because of dissatisfaction with how things are currently done, or the need to evaluate a recent innovation. The focus could be very narrow, as in a desire to see whether aged BBC microcomputers are sufficiently valuable to retain for some pupils, or wide, as in the effectiveness of the total provision of special needs ICT provision across an entire school or college.

One example of the implementation of such an approach is given in an article by Radcliffe and Hegarty (2001). A unit for young people with autistic spectrum disorders wished to evaluate its use of individual planning (IP). The published unit policy was scrutinized to produce a list of the features of this process that were supposed to happen (for example, 'every individual should have an IP meeting three months after admission and annually thereafter'). The manager suggested that if these were achieved at least 75 per cent of the time, that would be a significant achievement. Records of individual planning multidisciplinary meetings over two years were then examined to see how far each component of the process actually had happened for eight users of the service. Findings were checked with staff members to see if the records were faithful to what had really happened. Elements of the individual planning process were then easily divided into two: those meeting the minimum quality standard and those not meeting it. The findings were not only interesting but gave clear pointers for changes to be made – either those elements of the process that were not occurring could be omitted in future, since they were contributing nothing, or they could be done in different ways to ensure they happened more often. In this case, reports were not circulated at least one week before each meeting, aims and objectives from previous meetings were not reviewed and, most importantly, objectives for clients that were identified in meetings were not incorporated in the day-to-day care programmes. Having identified these difficulties, administrative and managerial procedures could be implemented to overcome them. Although this audit approach was applied in this example to individual planning, the method is adaptable to any aspect of an organization.

Consultancy and change

Seale (1993) designed her AMMASE checklist so that it would be possible to provide feedback to an organization on which specific aspects of their ICT were strong and weak. OFSTED inspections, as well as having a regulatory function, also provide feedback. Schools and colleges preparing for ICT inspections can use the publications by Stevenson (1997), National Council for Educational Technology (1997) and Hardy (2000) to alert them to key quality indicators. To effect change after an inspection is not easy. It can be helped by having people within the institution with sufficient influence to mobilize goodwill, change attitudes and lead on how existing ways of doing things can be modified to bring about new service outcomes. If resources allow, experts external to the organization may be brought in to help. In both of these two scenarios, whether the 'change-agent' is internal or external to the organization, a way of conceptualizing the relationship between change-agent and relationship is needed.

The idea of an 'ICT-capable school', suggested by Kennewell *et al.* (2000), took the view that schools are 'corporate entities that can think and act intentionally'. From their perspective, an organization is much more than the sum of its parts: it has a life and a mind of its own. Murgatroyd (1988) sees close parallels between the process of working with clients in a counselling encounter and that of working with a school to effect change. Summarizing his approach, he says: 'Effective consulting is a sophisticated form of counselling' (p. 66). The parallel comes closest in systemic family counselling, when the family is seen as an organization comprising interlocking and interdependent systems:

> . . . the behaviour of a family cannot be explained simply in terms of some summation of the behaviour of the individual family members . . . the culture of the family is all-important in shaping the thoughts, feelings and behaviour of family members. Given this realisation, family therapists have had to develop a theory of families *as organisations*.
>
> (Murgatroyd 1988: 68)

Teachers and managers in schools may find such concepts helpful, as they suggest that, given the appropriate situation, one person can bring about considerable change in the organization of a school. Someone well placed to do this kind of work would be the ICT coordinator. In many schools, people occupying this role work with colleagues supporting them with expert opinion. With the appropriate support, much useful change could be effected following audit exercises, at low cost, with such in-house consultancy. Change, however, is likely to require considerable staff development and support.

Teachers as researchers

Seale (1998) emphasizes the crucial importance of support for members of staff using ICT. Support could be practical, as in providing the appropriate resources. It should also be interpersonal, with colleagues and managers supporting emotionally and ideologically what individuals are doing so that innovations are encouraged.

For several years now, teachers attending courses designed to support the use of technology with learners with special educational needs at Keele University have undertaken small-scale research projects as part of their course work. A key aim of the course is to support teachers in carrying out 'action research' projects in their place of work. The development of these projects follows a protocol designed to encourage ownership of the project by school or college managers (to avoid the problem of the work being seen as 'only' a coursework requirement for the teacher), and a priority is placed on the project being valuable to the day-to-day work of the school or college. Projects completed during the past five years of the course have been of four main types:

1. *Audit projects*: a methodical survey of the level and quality of ICT provision at the level of the classroom or school.
2. *Courseware development projects*: production of prototype new software, WebPages or other course materials for individual children, or groups of children.
3. *Software evaluation*: systematic evaluation of one or more software products, usually comparing two examples of software of a particular kind.
4. *Precision teaching/systematic instruction projects*: detailed work with one individual learner in which a particular ICT-related skill was taught using systematic instruction methods.

An example of a research project was that conducted by Rachel, project worker at an integration project for adults with learning disabilities in London. She wanted to encourage her pupils to look at websites connected with their interests as a way of motivating them to work at literacy skills. She developed a simple but systematic method for identifying sites with her pupils that might be interesting to them, helped them to access sites and then encouraged them, for example by copy typing, or copying and pasting pictures into a Word document, to produce a short 'assignment' on each one. The resulting report of this simple but effective piece of action research was later edited to produce an article for a professional journal (Johnson and Hegarty 2003).

An example of the fourth category of research project is a study conducted by a final-year undergraduate student taking a course in educational psychology, Michelle Berry. A 9-year-old pupil at a school for children with physical disabilities was keen on using her laptop, but needed much assistance from a teacher. Michelle realized that the pupil could become more independent in using it if she could be encouraged to master switching the computer on, loading an application and, finally, logging off. She then followed a sequence of individualized instructions as follows:

1. Develop a good working relationship with the pupil.
2. Identify a psychomotor task that would be achievable, useful to the pupil and recognized as valuable by the teachers.
3. Complete a task analysis.
4. Devise a criterion level of attainment for the whole task and the sub-tasks.
5. Teach the task step by step, with errorless learning. This is achieved by giving as much assistance ('prompts') to the learner to complete the task as he or she needs, but no more.
6. Record the level of prompts given for each teaching 'trial'.
7. Progressively reduce the prompts as the child learns.
8. Maintain a relaxed and 'fun' atmosphere at all times that also conveys to the child the success he or she is making.

Working in this way, nine essential steps were identified, starting with asking the class teacher's permission to use the computer, through switching on, logging on, loading a word-processing application that the pupil liked and, finally, shutting the computer down correctly. Over 10 short sessions of teaching, the pupil went from minimal independent achievement on these tasks to being able to do most of them with very little encouragement to maintain her confidence. With more practice her confidence will grow further.

Experience of working with teachers on such projects shows that to initiate and complete even a small-scale project while working full-time as a teacher (often with additional ICT coordinator duties) is a tremendous undertaking. To complete the work, they need not only personal commitment but also the support of their managers. The achievements of course participants is an outcome of their decision to undertake a diploma course, the support of their place of work (both colleagues and managers), the structure of the course which requires action research and development projects to be done, and the support and expertise of course staff who are acting as project managers, supporters and consultants.

Will teachers not undertaking accredited courses do classroom-based research on ICT? Earlier in this volume it was argued that a collaborative venture between teachers and researchers was essential to innovation. Conditions will need to be right for research of any kind to flourish. Teachers need motivation, support and leadership. Schemes such as the Becta ICT Research Bursaries, announced in 2002, aim to give cash awards to teachers to undertake classroom-based research (Becta 2002d).

Conclusions

This chapter has reviewed a number of innovations and set out a series of key skills and perspectives that ICT professionals should acquire and practise if ICT is to be used effectively to support learners with special educational needs. The difficulty of demonstrating, objectively, by scientifically designed evaluation studies, that a particular innovation is effective makes it imperative that teachers are alert to innovations, make an effort to try to them out in their school, and conduct internal audits of effectiveness in collaboration with colleagues. A creative approach to supporting and managing staff may bring massive increases in the quality of ICT provision for individual pupils with little increase in resource cost. If, in addition, they can publicize their views to the wider teaching and research community, so much the better. A simple and effective way to do this is by the e-mail discussion list SENIT (see National Grid for Learning 2002b).

Finally, it is worth asking where do innovations come from? Teachers are better placed than anyone to come up with new ideas that can benefit pupils and colleagues. To progress an idea requires a team approach between teachers and producers – perhaps all schools can make it one of their future strategic objectives to develop liaisons with software producers and equipment designers.

References

Abbott, C. (ed.) (2002) *Special Educational Needs and the Internet: Issues for the Inclusive Classroom*. New York: Routledge.

Abbott, C. and Cribb, A. (2001) Special schools, inclusion and the World Wide Web – the emerging research agenda, *British Journal of Educational Technology*, 32(3): 331–42.

Acting Up (2002) *Acting Up's Multimedia Profiling: An Aid to Person Centred Working* (http://www.acting-up.org.uk/): accessed 5 December 2002.

Arnold, T., Cayley, S. and Griffith, M. (2000) *Video Conferencing in the Classroom*. Exeter: Devon Curriculum Services.

Atherton, T. (2002) Developing ideas with multimedia in the primary classroom, in A. Loveless and B. Dore (eds) *ICT in the Primary School*. Buckingham: Open University Press.

Award Scheme Development and Accreditation Network (2002) *ASDAN Home Page* (www.asdan.co.uk): accessed 5 December 2002.

British Educational Communications and Technology Agency (2002a) *Where Do I Start?* (http://www.becta.org.uk/start/index.html): accessed 6 December 2002.

British Educational Communications and Technology Agency (2002b) *ImpaCT2* (www.becta.org.uk/research/reports/impact2/index.html): accessed 5 December 2002.

British Educational Communications and Technology Agency (2002c) *Creativity in Digital Video Awards* (www.becta.org.uk/teaching/creativityawards): accessed 5 December 2002.

British Educational Communications and Technology Agency (2002d) *Becta ICT Research Bursaries* (www.becta.org.uk/news/pressrelease/2002/june2research.html): accessed 19 May 2003.

Department for Education and Skills (2002a) *SEN – Excellence for All* (http://www.dfes.gov.uk/sen/): accessed 6 December 2002.

Department for Education and Skills (2002b) *Young People and ICT: Findings from a Survey Conducted Autumn 2001*. London: DfES.

Dimitriadi, Y. (2001) Multimedia authoring with dyslexic learners, *British Journal of Educational Technology*, 32(3): 265–75.

Fawkes, S., Hurrell, S., Peacey, N. *et al.* (1999) *Using Television and Video to Support Learning*. London: David Fulton.

Global-Leap (2002) *Global-Leap.com: The Videoconferencing Directory* (www.global-leap.com): accessed 5 December 2002.

Goldman, S.R., Semmel, D.S., Cosden, M.A. *et al.* (1987) Special education administrators' policies and practices on microcomputer acquisition, allocation and access for mildly handicapped children: interfaces with regular education, *Exceptional Children*, 53(4): 330–9.

Hardy, C. (2000) *Information and Communications Technology for All*. London: David Fulton.

Hegarty, J.R., Bostock, S.J. and Collins, D. (2000) Staff development in information technology for special needs: a new, distance-learning course at Keele University, *British Journal of Educational Technology*, 31(3): 199–212.

Howitt, C. and Mattes, J. (2002) The British Museum COMPASS Website and learners with special needs, in C. Abbott (ed.) *Special Educational Needs and the Internet: Issues for the Inclusive Classroom*. London: Routledge.

Johnson, R. and Hegarty, J.R. (2003) Websites as educational motivators for adults with learning disability, *Brititsh Journal of Educational Technology*, 34(4): 479–86.

Kennewell, S., Parkinson, J. and Tanner, H. (2000) *Developing the ICT-Capable School*. London: RoutledgeFalmer.

Lewisham Borough Council (2002) *T@lent ICT Training for Teachers: Special educational needs and ICT* (http://ecs.lewisham.gov.uk/talent/pricor/sen.html): accessed 5 December 2002.

Loveless, A. and Dore, B. (2002) *ICT in the Primary School*. Buckingham: Open University Press.

Murgatroyd, S. (1988) Consulting as counselling: the theory and practice of structural counselling, in H.L. Gray (ed.) *Management Consultancy in Schools*. London: Cassell.

National Grid for Learning (2002a) *National Grid for Learning Home Page* (www.ngfl.gov.uk/index.jsp?sec=1&cat=0): accessed 5 December 2002.

National Grid for Learning (2002b) *Inclusion and SEN Discussion Areas: Becta-Supported Mailing Lists: SENIT* [Special Educational Needs – Information Technology] (www.becta.org.uk/inclusion/discussion/senit. html): accessed 5 December 2002).

Radcliffe, R. and Hegarty, J.R. (2001) An audit approach to individual planning, *British Journal of Developmental Disabilities*, 47(2): 87–97.

Seale, J.K. (1988) A study of microcomputer usage in an occupational therapy unit for adults with severe learning difficulties, in C. Bell, J. Davies and R. Winders (eds) *Aspects of Educational and Training Technology, Vol. XXII: Promoting Learning*. London: Kogan Page.

Seale, J.K. (1993) Microcomputers in adult special education: the management of an innovation. PhD Thesis, Keele University.

Seale, J.K. (1998) Management issues surrounding the use of microcomputers in adult special education, *Innovations in Education and Training International*, 35(1): 29–35.

Seale, J. (2001) The same but different: the use of the personal Home Page by adults with Down Syndrome as a tool for self-presentation, *British Journal of Educational Technology*, 32(3): 343–52.

Stevenson, D. (1997) *Information and Communications Technology in UK Schools*. London: The Independent ICT in Schools Commission.

Tizard, J. (1964) *Community Services for the Mentally Handicapped*. Oxford: Oxford University Press.

Widgit Software (2002a) *Widgit Software Home Page* (http://www.widgit.com/): accessed 6 December 2002.

INDEX

accommodations, 2, 36, 40
ACE Centres, 26–7
action research, 136, 141
adaptation, *see* accommodation
adaptations, 14
adaptive devices, 15
adaptive testing, 49–50
assessment, 16–17, 46–63
assistive devices, 14, 35
assistive technology, 15, 35–6, 38, 82
audit tools, 137–8
augmentative communication, 89

BBC, 23, 80
Becta, 18, 30–2, 129, 132
braille, 22
British Computer Society, 22

cerebral palsy, 37, 80, 82, 86
classroom management, 93
collaborative learning, 74–5
combining media, 131
COMPASS, 130
computer assisted instruction, 11

computer based assessment, 4, 17, 46–63
Curriculum, 2000, 33
curriculum based assessment, 4
customized keyboards, 3

digital cameras, 130
digital video photography, 132
Disability Discrimination Act, 41
Down syndrome, 131
dyscalculia, 54
dyslexia, 50, 57, 65, 130

e-Buddies, 16
Education Act (1981), xi, 37, 40
Education Reform Act (1988), 27, 40
enabling technology, 35, 96
    see also assistive technology
epilepsy, 81
evaluation, 133
exploratory learning environments, 12–13, 18

ICT, definition of, 8
ICT capability, 129

ICT and SEN
  history of, 4
  management of, 5, 17–18
IEP, 17, 111–27
IEP Writer, 113–27
ImpaCT2, 133–4
inclusion, 9, 36–7, 43, 45, 81
individual planning, 139
individualized learning, 11
innovation, 128
integrated learning systems, 4–5, 11, 48,
  64–79
Internet, 13, 16–17, 36, 43, 129

joystick, 105

keyguards, 44

learning difficulties, 13, 81, 96–8, 100,
  102–8
literacy, 65, 57–9, 60–70

Microelectronics Education Programme,
  23
Microelectronics Education Support Unit,
  24–7
multimedia, 130
multimedia profiling, 132

National Council for Education
  Technology, 27,30
National Curriculum, 2, 17, 27–8, 40
National Grid for Learning, 29–30, 33, 41,
  129
networked communication, 15–16, 48
numeracy, 65

outreach, 90–2
overlay keyboards, 15, 44

physical impairments (or disabilities), 14,
  37–8, 55, 87, 91

P-scales, 114
profound and multiple learning
  difficulties, 87

self-esteem, 72–3
SEMERC, 23–6
SENCO, 17, 40, 47, 109, 111–12
SENDA, xi, 42
sensory impairment, 14, 55, 81
Special Educational Needs
  Code of Practice, 4, 8, 16, 40, 42, 47,
    109–13, 115, 121
  definition of, 1, 8–9
  equal opportunity, 10
specific learning difficulties, 11, 13
spina bifida, 2–3, 86
staff development, 5, 91
  INSET, 24–5, 31
statement of special educational need, xi,
  17, 37, 39
switches, 14–15, 36, 84–7, 89
symbol processors, 44

target setting, 17, 114, 116
teaching machine, 65
text-to-speech, 44
touch screens, 14, 44
trackballs, 44
transition, 18
tutor, 11–12

video projectors, 131
videoconferencing, 3, 94, 132
virtual environments, 5, 12–13, 96–108
visual impairment, 2
voice recognition systems, 53
voice synthesiser, 3, 82

web-based curriculum, 18
word banks, 44
World Wide Web, 2–3, 14
writing skills, 13

SPECIAL EDUCATIONAL NEEDS, INCLUSION AND DIVERSITY
A TEXTBOOK

Norah Frederickson and Tony Cline

This book has the potential to become *the* textbook on special educational needs. Written specifically with the requirements of student teachers, trainee educational psychologists, SENCO's and SEN Specialist Teachers in mind, it provides a comprehensive and detailed discussion of the major issues in special education. Whilst recognising the complex and difficult nature of many special educational needs, the authors place a firm emphasis on inclusion and suggest practical strategies enabling professionals to maximise inclusion at the same time as recognising and supporting diversity.

Key features include:

- Takes full account of linguistic, cultural and ethnic diversity unlike many other texts in the field
- Addresses the new SEN Code of Practice and is completely up to date
- Recognises current concerns over literacy and numeracy and devotes two chapters to these areas of need
- Offers comprehensive and detailed coverage of major issues in special educational needs in one volume
- Accessibly written with the needs of the student and practitioner in mind

Contents
Introduction – Part one: Principles and concepts – Children, families, schools and the wider community: an integrated approach – Concepts of special educational needs – Inclusion – Special educational needs: pathways of development – Part two: Assessment in context – Identification and assessment – Reducing bias in assessment – Curriculum based assessment – Learning environments – Part three: Areas of need – Learning difficulties – Language – Literacy – Mathematics – Hearing impairment – Emotional and behaviour difficulties – Social skills – References – Index.

528pp   0 335 20402 3 (Paperback)   0 335 20973 4 (Hardback)

SPECIAL EDUCATIONAL NEEDS IN THE PRIMARY SCHOOL
A PRACTICAL GUIDE

Jean Gross

. . . extraordinarily rich in ideas . . . an essential buy.

Times Educational Supplement

. . . has proved especially influential at practitioner level . . . never failing to offer a balanced assessment.

British Journal of Special Education

I have a comprehensive library of books on special educational needs but I use this one more than any other because I find it readable, practical and accessible. It is a useful and informative book both to read cover to cover and to dip into. Although it is based on sound theoretical knowledge, it is clear that Jean Gross is writing from her own experience as a teacher and SEN practitioner.

Times Educational Supplement

Recent legislation and cutbacks to central support services mean that the responsibility for meeting special educational needs is resting ever more squarely on the shoulders of ordinary classroom teachers. Yet few feel wholly confident in their ability to adapt work within the national curriculum to meet the whole range of needs, or coordinate successful individual education plans for children who, for whatever reason, are not learning as well as they might.

This book will increase that confidence. Aimed at busy class teachers, special needs coordinators, heads and teachers in training, it shows how the teacher can build differentiation into planning lessons and schemes of work. It describes workable strategies for managing the most common behaviour difficulties and meeting special needs in language, literacy and mathematics.

At a whole school level, it offers practical guidance on reviewing special needs policies, assessment, record keeping, and the management of roles and resources. The focus is on the way in which schools can do a good job in meeting special needs themselves, within the everyday constraints of time, money and energy, and in so doing provide genuinely inclusive opportunities for all children.

This edition has been comprehensively updated and rewritten to cover the revised SEN Code of Practice and related legislation, new directions in inclusion and all the major curriculum initiatives now in place in primary schools.

Contents
Current perspectives on special educational needs – Developing and reviewing a whole school policy – Special needs and the national curriculum – Assessment and special educational needs – Action planning and record keeping – Making provision: finding the time – Making provision: using additional adult support – Managing behaviour – Communication and classroom relationships – Special needs in speaking and listening – Special needs in reading – Special needs in writing – Special needs in maths – Including children with complex needs – Resources – References

272pp   0 335 21217 4 (Paperback)

PLAYWORK
THEORY AND PRACTICE

Fraser Brown (ed.)

Children learn and develop through their play. In today's world the opportunities for that to happen are increasingly restricted. The profession of playwork seeks to reintroduce such opportunities, and so enable children to achieve their full potential.

This book brings together many leading names in the playwork field, to produce a text that has something for everyone. The in-depth exploration of a range of theoretical perspectives, will appeal to both playwork students and practising playworkers. Experienced practitioners offer sound practical advice about ways of improving playwork practice. There are chapters on the role of adventure playgrounds (past, present and future); the challenge of starting a playwork section in a local authority; and the value of networking. Contributors explore the essence of play; the historical roots of playwork; and the role of play cues in human and animal behaviour. There is an exploration of the astounding impact of a therapeutic playwork project on the development of a group of abandoned children in Romania. The final chapter reinforces the need for playworkers to be reflective practitioners in all aspects of their work.

Contents

Introduction – Part one: The roots of play and playwork – The essence of play – Making play work: the fundamental role of play in the development of social relationship skills – Towards playwork: an historical introduction to children's out-of-school play organizations in London (1860–1940) – Part two: Theories of playwork – Compound flexibility: the role of playwork in child development – Play deprivation, play bias and playwork practice – Towards a psycholudic definition of playwork – Part three: Putting theory into practice – the reflective practitioner – Professional playwork practice – Adventure playgrounds in the 21st century – Establishing play in a local authority – It's not what you know, but who you know! – Playwork in adversity: working with abandoned children – Playwork as reflective practice – Bibliography – Index.

224pp   0 335 20944 0 (Paperback)   0 335 20945 9 (Hardback)

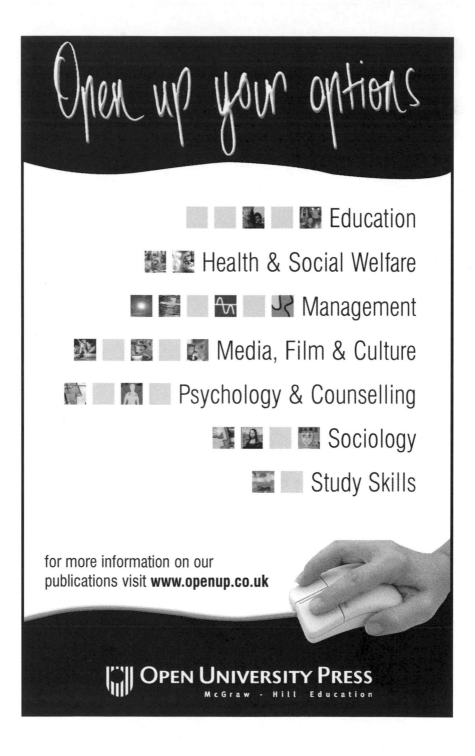